HOW YOUR CAT
CHOSE YOU!

TABLE OF CONTENTS

If You Like Someone, You Just Know

OUR EYES MET AND I FLIPPED

Have you ever stopped and wondered why that is? Or you might tell a friend 'I have a funny feeling about her…' which later proves to have been founded. Eyes are always meeting in crowded rooms and getting that certain knowing.

We pick up information peripherally about people. Most of this process is unconscious. The Romany gypsies say a woman knows by her first smell of a man if he is to be her future husband. We do activate actual chemistry when we speak of the chemistry between people. And probably smells, sounds and body language.

It not only applies to people, because we evaluate *things* in a similar way. When buying a house, very often one 'sets one's heart' on it. Without knowing why, there are factors on a deep subconscious level telling you to do or buy something. Intuition is very powerful and whether or not we want to give them credence, hunches instigate most of our decisions.

1

PREMONITIONS

But they are not just whims of fancy, plucked out of the ether by our wandering random brain. Premonitions result from sound observation and information-gathering. The explorers of old relied too on science rather than guesswork. Just because the prediction mechanism is not understood fully, means not that it is less accurate but rather that all the variables cannot, because we have such limited brainpower, take them all into account. Science and mathematics attempt to organise these variables one at a time and measure their effect, missing the point sometimes that they effects are grouped, with group dynamics of their own and which cannot be measured, only felt to be true on some deeper 'spiritual' level.

Scientists themselves have hunches anyway, and that is how their own hypotheses are set out in the initial stages of any experiment. The whole 'scientific method' is not even scientific. It is widely accepted that powers of intuition are present throughout the animal world. We say 'instinct' when we see baby animals stand, run and hunt. It is evident that an animal knows what it is doing from one minute to the next and it doesn't

get the information to do so from studying library books on animal behaviour.

CATS ARE SMART

Your cat is obviously no fool, but a highly intelligent animal being. In fact it is the most successful land-based killer, a species 35 million years old. Anyone on the earth 10 million years ago would have seen the African Wildcat walking around, looking exactly like today's average pet pussy.

So what is such a smart creature doing in your house? Well, it chose you, as you would choose a car or clothes. It selected you and your house for reasons you may be totally unaware of. In our human vanity we like to think we know everything, are in control and can determine and arrange outcomes. We like to think we chose the cat, but in keeping and observing this animal, we are reminded by them that there is another side. It's gonna cost us.

Cats know what they want and how to get it. They know who is easy to manipulate around their little paw and who isn't. How do they know? Because the cat appears more intuitive than we seem to be, and just as one often reads of fantastic exploits whereby cats can cross continents to get back home, so they can tell what house is their Soul-house.

It goes in reverse too. You think you chose your cat. Why did you think that? It has less to do with *your* character than the cat's. You were *made* to think that. All part of the cat's plan.

Yet what exactly is choice? Much philosophy has been written about freewill versus determinism. The discussion revolves around whether or not we really choose or put things down to fate. The simple fact overlooked is that when you feel you have a choice, then you have a choice. And when you feel you have no choice, then you don't! People will say both at different times. They will say they felt they had a choice of what biscuits to buy, but they felt they had no choice when it came to acting once in self-defence. Choice is a feeling, not something cognitive. The more we are in touch with our feelings, they closer we are to making choices that are right for us.

Personalities always work together as a complimentary team. This creates harmony. Cats seek harmony like no other animal. They know that *after* harmony will come food. It is a flawless system, and you have to admire them for it.

Some say cats are selfish. Those who do are often dog-lovers, anxious to promote their species-preference. Very often these folk have competitive personalities, and have a dog so they can be master of something.

But before we cite cats for selfishness, aren't we the same? We only do things for the pay-off; if not now, then later in some way. We go to some pains to ensure our selfishness isn't that obvious, because of our need to be social and being liked and admired. Cats have no such restrictions. If they aren't liked, they'll just up and go to where they are.

The counselling industry has nowadays gained medical respect. There is an ongoing interest in the differences between people and how we both differ or conform. Somewhere between character and appearance is our personality, or how our behaviour impacts on others. We are fascinated by what makes us tick and we will talk endlessly to anyone who is willing to listen about our favourite subject – ourselves!

UNIVERSAL RULES OF ATTRACTION?

There are a number of general tendencies identified by Newcomb in his studies of all acquaintance processes, including:

1. Proximity/attraction: We like others who are close by

2. Mere exposure: We like others whom we have been exposed to repeatedly

3. Reciprocity: We like those that show they like us

4. Basking in reflected glory: We seek to associate with those who are successful and prestigious.

5. Similarity/attraction: We like others who seem in some way similar to us, and

6. Complementarity-of-needs: We like others who possess qualities we don't have.

In this, the last and arguably the most important as a self-evaluation maintenance model, we prefer to associate with beings who do not outperform us in areas that are very relevant to our self-esteem. These are beings, human and otherwise, who by our evaluative definition are our complimentary opposites. The basis of interpersonal relationship-studies is that relationships do polarise. Partners take opposite ends of whatever issue may be in the air. They do that because it makes life interesting. It is human nature. A loud man will match up with a softly spoken woman. A short woman with a tall husband. The rowdy brother may have a meek sister. A mum will often say, "I can't understand my children: they're as different as chalk and cheese!"

The Greeks knew that that you give a woman and a man the same note to sing, each will sing it exactly an octave apart. Men and women naturally harmonise. There is one school of thought that attraction between the sexes is based on vocal properties, like talking speed, frequencies and pitch –

there is strong evidence that a man's average speech pitch may either be at the same musical note as his prospective partner's average speech or at a harmony of it.

Perhaps relationships are indeed like the flow of water; quick to establish some equilibrium in nature. In a tilting water tank, at one end the water will go up whilst the other goes down. It is the same between people, and between cats and people.

To see ourselves best is to see ourselves reflected in our spouses, our children and in our cats. Of these three, cats are the easiest to gain character reflections from because speech isn't in the way.

In short, it is not too far-fetched to look at yourself and see what kind of cat best suits you, and to look at your cat and see yourself.

SEARCH FOR THE AVERAGE

Individuals come in many shapes and sizes. Is there an average cat? Well, is there an average human? Normal is not necessarily average. We talk of normal/abnormal in the sense of good and bad, whereas average is the result of measurement. It is possible for a normal child to be below average, fairly happily. He is not as great a worry to his parents as the child considered to be abnormal although average. 'Normal' is subjective and arbitrary. It all depends on who is passing judgement.

Measurements need not be taken, and even when they are they can be of doubtful use. The 'average person' is a myth. Here are the physical characteristics of the average American male. He is aged 32, is 179cm tall and weighs 150lb. His chest measures 980mm and his waist 810mm. Shoes: 250cm. These are seven obvious dimensions. Of course there are other parameters. If we were to set out on a search for an actual person to fit these measurements we would be disappointed. Only 25% of the population would have any *one* of these measurements. And only 3.7% would have three of these so-called averages.

In fact, using the formula P/7 (where P = population), only 100 men out of 200,000,000 would show seven average factors. For eight dimensions we would uncover 20 and for nine dimensions – no one. As we all possess more than nine dimensions, there is no one in America or anywhere else who, by the law of averages would be a truly average man.

Then why do we use the word? Even though a true average doesn't exist in a full sense, it can provide a handy yardstick to look at individual differences and to construct hypothetical intelligence and personality tests based on the notion that people can be broadly categorised as 'types'. When we have the types mapped, we can better understand ourselves because the patterns of our behaviour can be matched with those of others we come to hear about. When recognising these patterns again, we find we can to some extent predict behaviour.

MODERN THEORIES

In the last two decades New Age Psychology has employed devices and oracles to describe preferences for the perception of the world. By changing one's outlook and internal language, one can change the way one perceives, thus helping to eliminate problems that have arisen from mis-perception. The labels have often been criticised as simplistic but that does not mean they are not useful.

Handedness is simplistic, most people doing things with both hands most of the time. It is in certain tasks that one hand seems to be preferred, and no-one knows exactly why. We seem to be born that way. In fact it would be rare to find a person who only used one hand all the time. I have a friend who writes with her right and throws a ball with her left, is ambidextrous in many ways but calls herself right-handed only because of the way she writes. Not too long ago, left-handed schoolchildren children were bullied into changing for the sake of homogeneity. Many became stutterers as a result.

These days there is less concern as to which hand a child writes with. What you do with the hand is more important.

It is the same with the categories 'left brain/right brain.' Left brain was supposed to refer to things logical, sequential, individualist and male; whereas right brain came to mean intuitive, collated, integrated, patterned, holistic and female. Most tasks are integrated anyway, and no-one was really suggesting they are not. It was a simple map dreamed up to explain differences in perception which seem to result in different behaviours.

Perceptual preferences are comfort zones and come about because we are gregarious and try to fit in with each other as best we can.

EITHER THE SAME OR REALLY DIFFERENT
In terms of compatibility it is generally desirable that you and your spouse are either very similar, or radically different. You and your partner will understand each other better, and have a respect because of either your sameness or your deep differences (which are obvious, delightful in the other's eyes, and entertaining).

The wife of evangelist Billy Graham is reported to have once said if a man and wife didn't argue, one of them would be unnecessary. Differences are important, forgivable, and can add to a relationship rather than detract. Relationships come apart when character roles are not as clear cut, and misinterpretations of the other person's behaviour can cloud one's perception.

A person who owns a cat is in a relationship with it, and the rules of relationship apply. What perceptual type you are will be reflected in the cat you find yourself with! That sounds scary, but that is why we have cats. In some way they mirror us. They seem to have the ability to be able to fill empty gaps in our lives through their subtle co-habitation techniques.

By looking at the categories of people as perceptual types, and categories based on physical characteristics, we can roughly describe the apparent character of an individual. These are age-old indicators of character, and under the term 'occult' has come palmistry, astrology and numerology. Under the term 'psychology' have come personality tests, IQs and other assessments. Sometimes unaware even to ourselves, we are analysing people we meet and with our neuro-packaging system we are coming up with quick read-outs as to whether or not we like them, can do business with them, or if they are future spouse possibilities. Go to any sales seminar and you will

discover that these techniques of quick analysis have now found their way to high levels in the sales world.

It is a vanity to think that humans employ these subtle methods and that animals would not. Dogs will bark at people they don't much care for – generally they are picking up on danger cues. Birds can sense what is a safe distance – for instance, ducks and geese will go much closer to small children.

Cats are no exception. They are masters at reading people who either come into their domain or whose domain they enter.

Just because the parameters are described here in isolation does not mean that they may not be summed together to provide a pattern. On the contrary, accuracy is enhanced the greater the array of relevant possibilities. We suggest the reader gathers as many variables as time allows, and match them to their locations.

HOUSES THAT CATS AVOID

There are some homes that hold no interest for cats. Unhappy elderly couples who argue a lot can drive cats away because of the noise they make with their relatively raspy voices.. Also, their houses can be invariably too tidy – (to their fastidious credit)there are few insects, rodents or smells, and hardly anyone eats much.

The same can be said for a house that has just welcomed home a new baby. Nobody will be prepared to pay much attention to a new animal as well and the screaming noises will deter. But that is not the case for a house with a toddler. Messy areas with toys on the floor are just up a playful cat's alley.

A cat will often avoid a house that has a teenage girl. Thirteen year old females typically go through a short period when they do not have high self-esteem. For them it is a time of heightened social awareness and they are looking for role models that are gregarious and pack-like, not independent and free-spirited as represented by a cat.

A home with a cat already resident will not be especially welcoming either. Nor a house with a dog who has been trained and reinforced for barking at anything within 100 miles that twitches a hair. A cat likes its territory all to itself, and gains its confidence from the integrity of the territory.

Then there are houses that have had a death occur, houses that get moved or renovated, houses with basements that are used for drum practice, overcrowded houses and houses without some form of heating.

Let us not forget too, houses that are vacuumed every day, houses that are too close to a busy road, and mobile homes. These hold little interest for cats who, to a man, look for regularity and a certain amount of peace.

Houses with no walls and no fence posts are avoided because they do not offer 'chinning' possibilities. Cats will know what I mean. Chinning is the action of rubbing the side of the head on flat or upright surfaces near you as you approach. It is the cat's way of marking the area with scent-gland secretions, as if to say, "this is my space now and you are welcome in it too."

Because cats bury their droppings on the edges of their range, they prefer some earth or hidden spots on boundaries between owners and neighbours. Apartments or flats that have only concrete yards and stone walls are not as favoured as those with vegetation.

HOUSES THAT CATS LOVE

Open plan, single-story bungalows or condo units are especially favourable. There are fewer doors and quick and easy access from sills to kitchen. Although cats do climb stairs, it is with trepidation and they prefer not to if given the choice. They like to have close access to the world outside, and unless upper stories lead to balconies and thence to trees, cats are a little suspicious of multi-storied structures.

Greenery is important, for shade and exploring shadows. Even if you have no garden, if there is flora and fauna nearby a cat will hang around your dwelling, given that other variables are to its liking.

Cats are flower enthusiasts, because flowers attract insects, insects attract birds, and cats hunt the birds.

Running water is a big draw-card. A small stream or dripping drainpipe, even a leaky outside hose-tap, holds endless fascination for a cat. It was noted in the early hybrid crosses that cats preferred to eliminate in running water, but today's breeds just seem to have ended up with an intrigue of it. Water-running might be then just an evolutionary vestige of a natural hygienic requirement. But there is a better reason. Hunting-cats have a better success rate because the sound of the water masks the hunter's stealthy approach. For this very reason hunting-cats prefer wet nights and use to their advantage the noise of heavy rain falling on the ground. Wet nights too bring the worms up, and the birds arrive. Just what cats like!

Dwellings that have outside waste bins or dumpers are where you will *always* find cats. Generally females outnumber males in these smelly areas by ten to one, males commonly having a greater tendency to mobility. In fact females

consider their territory to be just a bit more than their own garden or bin, while males have three to ten times as much.

Finally, a house that has an outside door with a cat flap in it will be chosen over a house without. Automatic access in and out of the home is not a new idea. Ancient doors have been discovered with cat-holes, for instance the old stable doors, so that the cats of old would have been able to keep stables rodent-free.

Let's begin to look now at basic types of people, and plot how a cat might be seen to adapt to each.

DO FAT PEOPLE HAVE THIN CATS?

There are exceptions to every rule, but on the whole, fat people do have thin cats. This is not meant to sound unkind. Overweight folk are more often poorer and can less afford quality food. That means even less to spend on the cat. Therefore the cat hunts to supplement what it is fed. Hunting is exercise. Exercise keeps you trim. Also, bigger people spend more time in the kitchen, which means the fridge door opens more frequently. The cat knows this and hangs around in the hope of gratification. Because these people can't run fast, they don't chase the cat away. Because the cat is always there, it doesn't get fed regularly, because it is assumed to be getting enough. By not having regular meals a cat is more likely to be undernourished.

Conversely a thin person will probably have a fat cat. The thin person rushes around a lot, is seldom there, and the cat gets used to being allowed the run of the house. This becomes more like the sleep of the house. It feels entitled to flop anywhere and spends its days basking in the conservatory. When the thin person arrives home, it is often in a state of guilt at having neglected the cat all day and in atonement the cat will get overfed.

If there is also a dog in the household, then the dog is most likely to be fat and the cat thin. Why? Because as people are always eating, titbits get spilt, and the dog enforces its more aggressive personality to get to the free goodies first. Therefore the cat has to be nimble, which means fit and slim, to get morsels and beat the dog.

If there is more than one human inhabitant of the house and they vary in dimensions, the rule seems to be that the dimensionality of the cat will be the opposite to that of its one special care-giver.

So for a tallish person, expect to see a cat that doesn't like staying on the ground. Tall people tend to have short-legged cats, who overcome any self-consciousness about it by climbing. Don't worry if the kitten goes up trees – it will find its own way down without you having to ring for a fire engine. Cat skeletons have never yet been found at the top of trees.

Short people have elegant cats which prance around for no apparent reason, spending much time walking to and fro to show off their supposed nobility.

Some large people call themselves big boned. Sometimes this is blamed on a cultural type, such as Hawaiian. But human bone sizes are mostly the same the world over, varying slightly between male and female. You only have to look at skeletons – most are identical. Fat-boneness is more a case of self-perception. If you think you are one of these, and that the extra weight you are carrying is a genetic thing, you will probably view your cat as a delicate creature who must be pampered. Such a cat will live an easy life, but a confused one. There will be many people in the house, coming and going. It will live mostly under the house and hunt at night, making noises and attracting other cats to its domain.

People of very slight build will attract a robust cat who will assume the role of mother over the human. Bits of birds and rodents may very well be dragged into the house as if to say *'This is how you hunt – I am teaching you because it is something you need to know'*

Having said all of the above, domestic cats do not differ as much in size and shape as dogs. The average cat height is 30cm at the shoulder, body length 45cm and a tail about 30cm long. There are two basic variations on body shape: the heavily built and the lithe. Breeders have sought to increase the fullness of the cobby shape in the British Blue, and at the other end of the scale accentuating the slimness of the modern Siamese. This is reflected in their skull shapes.

HUMAN'S SIZE	
OVERWEIGHT	Cat will need to be a good hunter.
SKINNY	An easy life, although a boring one.
TALL	Cat will be a tree and roof climber.
SHORT	Cat won't sit still for too long.
BIG-BONED	Cat can do no wrong.
SLIGHT	Owner needs mothering.

CAT'S SIZE	
FAT	Owner will be thin, often absent, and indulgent.
THIN	Owner will be slow and gluttonous.
SHORT LEGS	Owner will be tallish, concerned, and walk with a detached air.
LONG LEGS	Small stature no-fuss owner, who tends to get embarrassed easily.

ARE YOU A LOOKER, A LISTENER OR A TOUCHER?

There are said to be three ways we perceive the world, visually, auditorally and through touch. Whichever we feel the most comfortable with, is our perceptual preference, and accordingly this sorts us into one of those three distinct categories.

THE VISUAL OWNER
THINKS THE CAT IS PART OF THE DÉCOR

If the owner dresses elegantly and immaculately with shiny shoes and newly ironed clothes, she will probably have a cat that she likes looking at. How things look is her prime concern. Colour will appeal as will posture, markings and expression. She will think of her cat as a showpiece, and may enter it in Cat Competitions.

The visual owner says things like:
* ❖ "I see!"
* ❖ "It looks as though we'll have to…"
* ❖ "It seems that…"
* ❖ "Imagine if we…"

This human will be the always busy type, because there is always so much to do to keep the place tidy, in case anyone should come visiting. She'll therefore like a cat that sits around a lot and looks good; in fact makes the house look like a home. The cat will be something she likes looking at. Details will be important – flecks on the fur, bits of mucous around the nose. The cat is regarded almost as a piece of precious ornamental furniture.

She will therefore also notice that the cat makes a lot of mess, and unless she is continually following the cat around, cleaning up after it, she imagines that the work will all get to be too much for her. She especially won't tolerate hairs deposited on her black business suit.

Somehow she copes however, because she is susceptible to what appearance is given out. She hates housework but is sensible enough to know it must be done to present a good face. She has many best friends and they drop in at any time. They must not see an unkempt house. But her perception is that the cat just doesn't care. It has a mind of its own and is inconsiderate and selfish. On the other hand, the cat's perception is that it should watch itself. The important thing is to look good and

preen. Also, there is someone prepared to clean up after me, whatever I choose to do. Mainly, all I have to do is be there.

And so the Visual Owner thinks the cat rules the house, because it does what it likes while she can't.

THE AUDITORY OWNER
THINKS CAT IS A SOURCE OF STORIES

The auditory owner dresses in plain styles and simple earthy colours like greys, whites, browns and blacks. She cares more about what people will say about her than what impression they have, and about what things sound like. Consequently she's also interested in what sound her cat makes, being drawn initially to a kitten with a soft meow.

It happens in reverse too. A kitten with a plaintive cry will detect empathy and direct itself toward a potential owner that displays that empathy in body language. This owner will love whatever sound the cat makes, and weave it into the fabric of her life.

A sweet shy meow will draw the owner in, whilst a Siamese, which is usually too vocal for its own good, can fare badly with an auditory owner. Moreover, auditory people want a cat to have a stable nature, not fickle like a Siamese can often be, up one minute and down the next. And Siamese cats tend to be erratic.

If the owner is softly spoken she will probably judge her cat to be a loud individual and lovingly call it a bully. The auditory person will remember what her cat does in intimate and gory detail, because she is a collector of stories. She will be able to hold court for hours in mixed company, going on and on about cat dramas.

The auditory person is usually intelligent and sometimes slow to get into a project because she does things one at a time and doesn't think there is a need to get stressed. She thinks her cat is a little dim at times. Because she is a loyal person and values fidelity, it is her observation that her cat will go off with others at the drop of a hat. Oh, she's not discerning, she'll go to anyone, is what you often hear. But cross the auditory person or let her down and she may explode with fury. Consequently many auditory people are said to have dual natures – placid and easy-going most of the time, but when pushed past their bottom line, a raging bull!

Most auditory owners find that their cat is something around the house with a more even keel, and therefore represents stability, something solid. They usually get upset themselves if their cat displays anger.

They are people looking for answers. Many are deeply religious or strongly linked to what they perceive to be a worthwhile cause. Some think that getting a cat is the answer. Sometimes it just comes down to the fact that they love talking and creatures around them who are prepared to listen!

THE KINAESTHETIC OWNER
THINKS CATS ARE FOR STROKING

The third type of owner is the feely-touchy person. Her clothing is not glamorous or formal, although she does have these in her wardrobe for special occasions, or for 'best'. She dresses for comfort, in slacks and wool when she can, and in soft shoes and sneakers. She may even choose a job that allows her this amount of dressing-down freedom. She is more concerned with how she feels about something or someone, than how something looks.

Words she will use will be:
- ❖ "I feel…"
- ❖ "I'm happy with that…"
- ❖ "I felt quite touched/shocked/pleased …"
- ❖ "It makes me so mad…"

She is looking for feelings from her cat. It doesn't matter that her feline is not a pedigree, and she hardly takes notice when it meows, because she fancies that all cats meow most of the time anyway.

Feelings to her are a sign of sincerity. She values truths, directness and even surprises good and bad. The Kinaesthetics love hugs and touching and acts of kindness and are generally very fond of all animals. They also detest insects. All that is mutually returned.

They are also sensitive and would prefer a nice fluffy cat that just sat there in empathetic silence, to one that looked showy but that got in everyone's hair, or one that did things that caused controversy. These people store past hurts, and dwell too much on anything gory.

They are trusting, perhaps too much, and although they might appear casual and laid-back, even flippant; they are deep thinkers. The lighter side is just a cover for their deep-seated concern about life and their sincerity. They are not looking for answers – they know the answer – that there should be more love in the world.

Kinaesthetic people make fine nurses, teachers, vets, conservationists, receptionists and missionaries. They also make good lovers, cooks and loyal friends. They are people who tend to remain alone after a marriage breaks up. A cat to them is good company – they make no demands – except that it *be* there.

COMBINATIONS

Most people are a combination of two of these three general personalities. Visual and auditory folk can be attention seeking, but not the kinaesthetic.

Visuals need stimulation but don't mind silence. Auditories can't stand silence, and will always say something if no-one has spoken after a pregnant pause. They are the ones who pipe up from the back about the weather in a crowded elevator.

Visuals speak fast and at a higher pitch than the others. Auditories speak in more measured tones, and lower, picking their words carefully. Kinaesthetics don't like talking much; they tend to be jerky and awkward and get nervous in front of a crowd. If you can hear her coming, she is probably a Visual. Although Auditories are quite capable of emitting healthy volume, it is seldom sustained for long periods.

Shyness is as unknown to the Visual person as confidence is to the Kinaesthetic. Auditory people are only shy if they are hesitant over what to say. If they are sure of their material, all apprehension vanishes, and they can't wait to get in front of that audience and tell them what they came to tell them. The Kinaesthetic person worries whether or not people care, either for them if in a close relationship or performing situation, or in a global sense.

Auditories sometimes wear colours that are too bright because they don't see dress balance as a visual thing. What an Auditory would call smart might be called by outlandish by a Visual. Often, an Auditory man will wear a 'loud' shirt. Such a person is really quiet and shy but is shy about his quietness! The loud shirt is his way of compensating. Often someone wearing loud clothes also wears sunglasses – they are getting the attention but it is a little too hard to handle.

Where the Visual person's voice is often shrill, the voice of the Auditory person is more modulated. Although this person may speak fast also, it is usually the more interesting voice. It is pleading and often plonky.

The speech of the Auditory person has points of emphasis, as if there are italicised words here and there. Kinaesthetic folk sometimes *only* speak as if in italics, and have been known to not finish sentences once the emphasised word has been uttered.

They might say:
- ❖ "What the…?"
- ❖ "Good God, if only…!"
- ❖ "Well I'll be…!"

In the main, kinaesthetic people speak to express feelings. Once that feeling has been transmitted, there is no need to continue vocalising. They may even grunt, like, "Uh huh," "oh," "tsk tsk," "ahem," "psst," and "shoo!"

On a hot day, the Visual person might say, "Isn't it hot today?" to somebody else, because the temperature of the room is perceived as an *appearance*. The Auditory person will say a straight-forward, "It's hot in here," or "I'm hot," for that's what she's *telling* herself. The Kinaesthetic person will just go "Phew!" to him/herself and sweat.

YOUR CAT KNOWS

So how do you know which of the three you are? By looking at your cat, of course!

- ❖ If your cat comes in and rubs her cheek on your leg you are probably Kinaesthetic.
- ❖ If your cat rubs her cheek on doorways near you, she is apprehensive, so you would be Visual or Auditory.

❖ If your cat leaps into your lap, you are clearly Kinaesthetic.

❖ If your cat leaps into your lap and purrs, you could be Auditory or Kinaesthetic but are unlikely to be Visual.

❖ If your cat leaps into your lap and starts pummelling, you are probably *not* Kinaesthetic.

❖ If your cat sits in the house in one spot for most of the day, you are probably Visual.

❖ If your cat spends most of her time around the kitchen or food-bowl, you are very likely Auditory.

❖ If your cat spends most of the day outside, you are Visual or Auditory.

❖ If your cat alternates between your bedroom, your office, and the sofa, you are more likely to be Kinaesthetic.

HOW DO YOU STAND?

Think of an 'S' shape. Imagine it is your spine, viewed from the side, with the body facing to the right. All postures can be described in terms of this 'S'. Actors use this schema for locating characters within *themselves*. By changing his posture the actor can 'feel' how a person of this or that body shape would perform in a given scripted situation. Rather than imagining being in someone else's shoes, he is imagining what his own reactions would be if the story happened to him.

The S line is measured as a function of the growth/development stages of a human being. To begin with, the child stands straight and confident. He is alive to new experiences. We call this Alert.

He gets older and cockier and puffs out his chest with his head back as if to say Look at me Mummy, aren't I clever! His arms are back and his chest leads the way. This position is called The Arrogant.

As this child gets older still, his height may be an embarrassment because people equate height with power and strength, which being young he doesn't feel. Adolescents get round shoulders, which is the top of the S starting to curl. We call this The Hunched.

With the advancing years this curl becomes more marked and the elderly typically lean right over with their heads looking toward the ground. This is The Stoop.

These postural types *do* cause changes in behaviour not only in those who exhibit them, but also in those who choose to be around them. Schoolteachers know that the slouched pupil will not be able to concentrate as easily as the one sitting up alert. His posture will also affects others around him and before long the whole class is asleep.

Whatever posture *you* exhibit will to some extent reflect how you see yourself, how you appear to others, and what set of behaviours your 'character' displays. Whatever cat you have will react to that character accordingly. Many find that just by consciously changing posture, they can virtually reinvent themselves.

THE ALERT POSITION

What we call 'alert' means in people terms extrovert, confident, brash, sensitive, workaholic, and often thin. These people walk erect and leaning forward, with paces that are often too long for their height. They have clear eyes and shortish hair, quick movements and may talk in a snappy way.

They want a cat to fit in with *their* lifestyle, another being that's a tad meek but at the same time, loving. Why anyone would *not* want to follow his path and example is beyond his comprehension Sometimes such a person can be hard to live with because she is perceived as making demands on a partner. Actually she has high standards and calls a spade a spade, and expects others to do the same. She wants a cat that is strong, can look after itself, but still be there as a companion.

THE ARROGANT POSITION

Arrogant people are not necessarily bullies, although they may appear so. This is often because they speak louder than the situation requires. They have a lot of pride, strive for achievement, value fitness and admire strength. Many are shorter than average, which contributes toward some insecurity. This factor makes a cat tense also.

Arrogant people need to see the results of success to feel okay. They are always seeking approval, which encourages a cat to be finicky. As they get older they may gain weight and slow down somewhat.

An arrogant owner may tend to speak louder than she necessarily has to. She may feel insecure if she is short. She may feel the need to succeed but really deep down knows she is a softie, and at times lonely.

Cats of these people are slightly fearful and dependent. They will want to come inside but will test the waters first.

THE HUNCHED POSITION

This type is shy, reserved, sensitive, an achiever and hard worker who wants the cat to pull its weight too. Reliable, honest, slightly too conservative, this is someone who doesn't like their cat doing an inappropriate act.

At times these people appear to be carrying the world on their shoulders, and the temptation is to offer to take some of the burden. If you did however, another burden would present itself, for this person's burden is generally of his own making.

These people are so careful that their personality borders on boring. They favour rituals and tried-and-true routines. Seldom are they wild risk-takers.

Their cats, however, are. The cat around the hunched person wants to play. It does cheeky and naughty things to gain attention.

THE STOOPED POSITION

Frail, introverted, soft-spoken and retiring, these folk don't have much energy for big tasks. They may appear chatty and outgoing, but in reality they often dream of being somewhere else in a different place and with different things happening. Hence they are often overly critical of the world as it is.

Nevertheless they are sincere and honest and make loyal friends. They are also generous to a fault. Cats in this house - and there are often more than one - are spoilt rotten!

POSTURE	
ALERT	Cats will cower and stay out of the way.
ARROGANT	Cats will act submissively.
HUNCHED	Cats will act saucy and flamboyant.
STOOPED	Cats run the house.

WHAT SHAPE IS YOUR FACE?

The face is said to be the map of the soul. What can be hidden by changing posture or voice cannot be as easily kept from a face. Although obviously racial/genetic characteristics play a large part in the structure, a person's face as they are growing becomes altered by the facial muscles that are brought into play through the expression of the most frequent emotions.

The round face of the happy bouncing child will stay a rounded face in adult life whereas the sombre and constantly fearful child may later become gaunt.

A rounded head, spherical, indicates someone easy-going, generous, open to new ideas and happy to have a good time. This person is very tolerant of whatever her cat does. This owner does not have to show off to feel accepted. Perhaps over-indulgence needs to be watched, as well as overindulging the cat, because this person is sometimes too easy-going and is often a push-over – a dream also for salespeople eager to sell something.

But contrast this to the thin narrow face, which is said to belong to someone more choosy, cautious and suspicious. According to gypsy lore, a long narrow face was untrustworthy. These folk would also be critical of their cats. There would be a whole range of things that their cat does that they would be distrustful and suspicious of. To a cat this would be viewed as encouragement and attention, and that set of behaviours would increase.

FACE OF OWNER	
ROUND FACE	Cats rule, don't learn limitation.
THIN, NARROW FACE	Cats do naughty things.

FACE OF CAT	
ROUNDED (E.G. PERSIAN)	Owner talkative and noisy.
TAPERED (E.G. SIAMESE)	Owner is a little slower, and not always openly affectionate.

PARTS OF FACE

EYES

As far as cats are concerned, the BEST owners' eyes are clear shiny and sparkling. Such an owner's cat will be wanted and cared for and treated as one of the family. If the eyes are large, the owner will be happy, innovative and generous. This, too, bodes well for a cat. On the other hand, small eyes indicate someone uptight and reserved. A cat with this person will be able to do what it likes, but it should not expect too much stroking to be forthcoming.

Spectacles are an indicator of intelligence. Cats are usually wary around those who know what they are up to, but they are also contented, because of mutual respect. Short-sightedness also indicates sensuousness and imagination in lovemaking. A cat can expect to be wooed for affection and will readily play along.

Round eyes mean the person is a hard worker. She will expect the cat to pull its weight and not make work for her.

If the person has one eye higher than the other, it indicates emotional ups and downs. This means the cat will need to be on an even keel and learn to treat outbursts from the owner as if it was water off a duck's back.

Crow's feet around the eyes means this person laughs easily. Her cat is a source of amusement.

Eyebrows meeting in middle indicate defiance. This person's cat does things which annoy her.

Eyes that are wide apart mean a tolerant owner who sees broader perspectives, whilst eyes narrow together indicate a tidy person, very reserved, and conscious of appearances, who will be restrictive and demanding when it comes to Miss Moggy.

If owner has bulging eyes, she is probably hypersensitive to emotions and lets her cat do its own thing because she not only doesn't understand it; she hasn't the time to find out what makes her cat tick. She is too busy trying to fix herself up anyway, plus the fact that she is not home a lot of the time.

Blinking indicates kindliness, someone with a soft voice. If it is too frequent it can point to mental instability. This will be a good house for a cat because of the sensitivity of such an owner.

Deep-set eyes are a sign of withdrawal. Such a person probably holds control over her emotions. She will view her cat as scatty or nervy, and her cat will keep its distance.

In terms of color, light brown means the person is unaffectionate and red means highly strung. Consequently these two eye-colours are not popular with cats. However, black(intelligence, decisiveness and sensuality), dark brown (loyalty to family), blue(variety) and green(nature-loving) are eye-colours cats find are easier to be around.

If the colours are intense, this indicates an active mind, which is also to the cat's liking as it means getting fed on time and an interesting house full of different smells.

EYES OF OWNER	
LARGE	Good home for cat.
ROUND	Restrictive environment.
SMALL	Expect less strokes.
ONE HIGHER THAN OTHER	Cat must learn patience.
WIDE APART	Owner is tolerant
NARROWER	Owner imposes limitations.
BLINKING	A kind owner.
DEEPSET	Cat is wary.
BULGING	Total freedom for cat.
BLACK, DARK BROWN, BLUE, GREEN	Good owners to be around.
LIGHT BROWN/RED	Doesn't bode too well for cats.
INTENSE COLOURS	Very good sign for cats.

EYES OF CAT	
LARGE	Owners introspective, cautious.
SMALL	House full of energy/noise, owners live fast & furious life.
BOGGLE, PROTRUDING	Owner leaves home for long periods.
EYES FAR APART	Owners annoyingly inconsistent.

CHEEKS

High cheekbones on the owner indicate a person unafraid to tackle difficult matters, but one who has few close friends and lacks affection. She has a cat around but she expects the cat to fare for food outside, as well as what she feeds it.

Hollow and sunken cheekbones mean an owner who has a hunger for wealth and power. She imagines her cat already *has* this power, and thinks that by watching her pet she will learn the secrets of success that she will be able to incorporate into her own life. She treats her cat well and pampers it.

A cat's cheeks tell a different story. Full and fleshy is a compliant, non-aggressive, comfort-seeking but quietly assertive cat, which will attach itself to an owner with a career. Thin hollow cheeks belong to a cat with a lonely unhappy owner.

MOUTH

The best human-mouth as far as cats are concerned is one that is horizontal where lips meet, and has corners that slope up. This indicates evenness, openness and balance. A cat in such a house will be treated fairly and looked after well.

A firmly closed mouth belongs to an owner who grits her teeth and tackles the big issues front-on. A person of courage who appreciates and respects, although she may perceive her cat as timid.

A mouth half-open is said to indicate the person who works at night and who likes sleeping-in. Cat may have to adjust hunting schedule.

The owner with a large mouth is a good leader who can inspire confidence and trust. She forgets malice quickly. She herself is passionate, and therefore notices that her cat tends to be cold-hearted.

A regular, so-called-glamorous aristocratic-shaped mouth is a sign of noble breeding and strong willpower. She could easily perceive her cat to be greedy and cowardly.

If owner's mouth is small, it indicates someone more easily satisfied sexually, but who will bottle up her problems rather than seek help. She is sure to think her cat whines too much for affection and attention.

A person who has cheeks swelled out and her mouth pushed forward probably has a career using her voice and jaw muscles, possibly a teacher, lawyer, or broadcaster. Around the home she will do the talking if there are other humans in the house. In this case her cat will be a non-talker. But if she lives alone, she will come home and give her mouth a rest – so her cat will be perceived as the talker.

A crooked mouth, that is, it goes up at one end, is a sign of deceit. It could also mean wariness and caution. However, she will perceive her cat to be deceitful too.

The straighter the horizontal line where lips meet, the more likely this person is to keep promises. She will therefore notice if the cat doesn't do what she has been trained for. A cat in this house can try for high status and please herself what she does, but there may be consequences!

If there is a wavy line however, where the lips meet, we have a person confident with words, a smooth talker, reliable, but who might not always enjoy financial stability. Cat will be rather quiet and be expected to be dependent on her at times, and independent at other times.

MOUTH OF OWNER	
HORIZONTAL	Cat will be treated fairly.
FIRMLY CLOSED	A safe house for a cat.
HALF-OPEN	Cat will get late breakfast
ARISTOCRATIC	Cat must take back seat.
LARGE	Cat could be smothered.
SMALL	Cat told to keep quiet.
CROOKED	Expect cat to be naughty.
STRAIGHT LIPS	Cat must keep to routines.
WAVY LIPS	Cat will be quiet and often confused as to expected role in the house.

MOUTH OF CAT	
LARGE	Cat forgets quickly, so owner gets away with small unkindnesses.
FULLY OPEN	Uncertain cat, owner probably has divided loyalties.
HALF OPEN	Owners will fuss, admire and spoil cat, not realising cat is out all night.
CLOSED	Cat is in control of house, gets what it wants.

NOSE

A person with a long nose is stubborn, with much self-pride. Conversely, she thinks her cat doesn't have much self-respect. She will not want closeness with her feline. If the nose is straight she is a good thinker, and the cat will enjoy her respect. If a crooked nose, the cat may be neglected somewhat.

Big nostrils indicate a person independent, adventurous and possibly mean and selfish. Once again, a cat should look to her own resources in this house. She will not be waited on hand and foot.

A plump nose indicates a hoarder, someone of wealth, especially if the nose is arched. The higher the arch, the better the fortune. Such a person is more fond of dogs, but tolerates cats. However, the spouse or partner will look after the cats' interests, quite likely in a secretive way.

Bumps on the nose indicate financial worries. Cat food may be meagre and plain.

A pointed nose means a chilly disposition but someone who is a fighter for people's rights. It also means someone kind to animals.

An eagle nose is a sign of cruelty. This person will not only expect beings to look after themselves, but may actually deliberately make it hard for them to do so.

Someone with a high nose seeks solitude and has difficulty accumulating wealth. But the cat will be her best friend.

A small nose indicates immaturity, difficulty saving money, moody disposition, and someone who lacks concentration to finish a task. She will seek a cat who is prepared to be independent. However, she enjoys her cat much as a child does, and people will not get too threatening in this house.

If a person has a twitch, it indicates suspicion. This person is a hard conscientious worker, who expects life to be rather disappointing and requiring hard work. She may resent what she perceives to be loafing.

The nose of the cat is the area of health and success. If attention is paid by the cat to this region, as in rubbing the nose with a paw or touching the owner with it, something is troubling. A sense of impending danger may be the case also, and an owner may well be advised to take caution.

NOSE OF OWNER	
LONG	Cat may have lonely existence.
BIG NOSTRILS	Cat must look after herself.
PLUMP	Watch out for dogs.
ARCHED	Spouse will be cat's meal-ticket.
STRAIGHT	Respect for cat.
CROOKED	Cat may be neglected.
BUMPS	Cat may roam looking for food.
POINTED	Cat will be protected.
EAGLE	Cat better be vigilant.
HIGH	Good house for a cat to be in.
SMALL	Cat will be played with.
TWITCHY	Cat should sleep in the sun away from the house.

NOSE OF CAT	
BROAD	Action, optimism, owner lazy.
LONG	Ambitious, proud, self-reliant, owner will be elsewhere though.
SQUASHED	Quiet cat, sometimes insecure.
GRAY, LIFELESS	Owner could be cruel.
SMOOTH	Healthy household.
EVEN-SHAPED	Owner is fair and consistent, indicating success and harmony.
SHORT	Playful cat, owners fun-loving.
POINTED	Too much curiosity. Owner tires quickly.
UPTURNED	Demands consistency. Anger if betrayed.

LIPS

Fleshy lips on the owner generally indicate sensuousness and warmth. This person will enjoy good health and will be kind to cats. She imagines that her cat can do without her and so goes a little out of her way to supply little treats every now and then. There will always be some sort of cooking going on.

Thin lips mean someone ambitious, with determination, who is more passionate about their job than the people in their life. There is a streak of what might be perceived as meanness. However, it is unintentional; it is just that the person's mind is on other things. She will expect her cat to be independent, so a cat would be expected to be self-reliant in this house. The cat will always be wanting more affection than the owner is prepared to give.

A tightly closed mouth indicates a desire for control of the self and for thoroughness. Sometimes little 'pull-in' lines are evident all around the sides and top and bottom of the mouth. This person may have been let down badly by someone, and her determination is very strong not to let it happen again. At times her cat is regarded as a nuisance, but at other times it is a welcome companion.

If the upper lip is thicker than the lower lip, the person is both naïve and devious. She is intelligent and strong-willed, and is likely to have more than one cat and even a dog as well, just to see them all perform together. A cat in this house won't be lonely for company, but won't get to spend much time with the owner.

Cats lips are difficult to see unless peeled back, so cat lip readings are less worthwhile.

LIPS OF CAT	
FLESHY	This house is Tidbit City.
THIN	Cat should not expect owner to be home much.
TIGHTLY CLOSED	Cat needs to check out if owner in a good frame of mind today.
THICKER UPPER LIP	Cat will have to compete with other animals or children.

TONGUE

At the turn of the century, German scientists and physicians thought of the tongue as a mirror that reflected the overall health of the patient. Recent research has proven that the back of the tongue harbours bacteria that can cause bad breath. By looking sat the tongue's appearance, diagnoses can be made about personality and general health.

Bad breath can mean money or relationship worries. Why? Anaerobic sulphur-producing bacteria live within the surface of the tongue and proliferate when toxins increase, due to depression or bad diet. Oral bacteria can trigger blood-clotting and inflame arteries, leading to heart disease. These are stress indicators, of which business and romance top the list, according to the Chicago Tribune.

Ancient folklore says the power of The Spirit is in the power of the Tongue. Things can't happen until they are first spoken. Apparently, Satan also is opting for the use of your power and wants to control your words. Without the use of your tongue he is helpless and bound. Evil thoughts can be visible in the way the tongue looks and moves. Words and sounds are eternal, and once spoken they will always exist. So care in words chosen, used to display carefulness in character. Thus, according to this theory, the way a tongue moves can indicate (or not) caution in personality.

If the tongue is lumpy, there could be a build-up of wastes; whereas a pitted tongue is said to mean confusion. White spots meant bad dreams and predicted foreboding. A strong flappy tongue denotes a person of high status, someone controlling and assertive.

A slow-moving or still tongue indicates submissiveness. If a dry appearance, this can mean bad diet due to the presence of antidepressants, alcohol, too much sugar, too much acid (fruit juices, coffee, tea is OK) or too much dairy food (thick proteins like beef and chicken).

A tongue protruding can be an attempt to rid the system of toxins.

TONGUE OF OWNER	
LONG	Passionate nature, assertive, sometimes cruel. Cat should exercise caution.
DRY	Owner not calm or contented; cat's role is to bring peace and healing.
FAST MOVING	Owner bossy, cat needs to take submissive tack.
SLOW OR STILL	Cat can exert influence and some measure of control.
LUMPY	Owner not well, cat must learn how to fend for itself.
PITTED	Cat will want routines established, and meals on time.
SPOTTED	Cat will feel the need to be vocal and to look on bright side.
BAD BREATH	Financial or romantic worries.

TONGUE OF CAT	
DRY	Good sign. Confident and happy.
FLICKING	Alert cat, curious, also could mean agitated and fearful of owner, or pet rivalry.
HANGING OUT	Owner neglectful in some way.

TEETH

If teeth are large and long, this is said to indicate long life. This person is likely to be health conscious, possibly vegetarian. She will give her cat the right diet, which means lots of meat, but it also means no tidbits. Sorry puss!

Well-arranged teeth means that the person learns quickly. She will be able to pick up on what her cat is trying to tell her, and be aware when something is wrong. A cat is lucky to have this owner.

When the top two teeth are very prominent and large, the person is said to be stubborn. Such an owner wants her own way and will not stand for a finicky cat. Take it or leave it, will be the attitude. This inspires a cat to co-operate if she wants to be fed.

If the teeth slope inwards, it means that the person is erratic and unpredictable. One minute the cat is the flavour of the month and the next minute it is ignored. The cat will want routines a little more adhered to.

Thick teeth belong to an excitable person, someone passionate and full of life. This makes for a calm animal. A cat is very loved by this owner.

On the other hand, thin teeth mean a fickle nature. A cat cannot place too much reliance on this person to deliver. Her cat will eat anything, because otherwise there may be nothing at all. There will probably be mice in or around the house though, because hygiene may not be up to scratch.

When the person's gums are visible when smiling, it is said to indicate a swinging from generosity to stingyness. The cat will have an even nature, even though sometimes there will be food in the bowl and often it will be late.

Protruding teeth mean a strong desire for approval. This owner will have a cat that doesn't care much. It may make noises at night and think nothing of jumping on a bed to wake someone so as to remind them it is hungry.

TEETH OF OWNER	
LARGE AND LONG	Cat will be well-fed.
WELL-ARRANGED	Cat is in a secure environment.
TOP TWO TEETH VERY LARGE	Cat won't get own way.
TEETH SLOPE INWARDS	Cat should not expect things on time.
THICK TEETH	Good bonding with owner.
THIN TEETH	Good hunting.
GUMS VISIBLE WHEN SMILING	Cat needs to tell owner when hungry.
PROTRUDING	Cat will be encouraged to be inconsiderate.

TEETH OF CAT	
WORN	Older cat, hunter, health worries impending.
WIDE	Energy and aggression. Owner absent too much.
STRONG, POINTED	Strong and confident but owner possibly weak.
LONG	Uncertain, owner making too many changes.
SMALL	Critical, argumentative, lacking in stimulation.
SHARP	Self-control, detached, healthy, in charge of own life. Owner around when needed.

CHIN

If owner's chin is prominent, the so-called Lantern jaw, this person is ambitious and moody. Problems about inner security in childhood are well behind and almost overcome. Cat will hunt but not particularly ambitiously.

When the chin recedes, there is little ambition; these people do not stretch themselves. But *this* owner's cat is brave, independent, and will take its hunting seriously.

CHIN OF OWNER	
PROMINENT	Hunting will be a hassle.
RECEDING	Good hunting prospects.

EARS

If a person's ears stick out, she needs to draw on her inner strength. In contrast, her cat is fairly stable.

If someone's ears are long, it is said to mean suspicious and cynical. A cat around will get under her feet all the time, so this owner imagines. Not a very pleasant cat environment.

The person with ears wider at the top excels in some subject. Her cat will be a good all-rounder.

Large ears indicate confidence. This person's cat will be of a timid nature, and whine at the slightest whim.

Small ears indicate a lack of confidence and a person with behaviours designed to hide this fact. Such an owner may make too much noise, hold parties and barbeques, and always fill the house with strangers. A cat in this house will be well used to strangers and go to anyone for a pat. Tidbits may well be around.

Thick ears indicate fortune and health. A person of generous nature, easy-going and playful. A good cat/owner relationship here.

Thin ears mean physical weakness and possible health problems, if not now or looming, then probably in earlier years. This person looks out for their cat's welfare, because health has been a focus in life generally. She may take the cat often to the dreaded(in the cat's eyes)vet.

Ears on a cat generally describe intelligence. In fact, Siamese were bred with bigger ears for that very reason. It does not mean that a cat with shorter ears will be the cat version of an idiot, but it probably won't be the most alert animal on the block.

EARS OF OWNER	
FLAT	Good fortune, long life.
STICK OUT	Cat contented with role in house.
ROUND	Wealth, kindness.
LONG	Cat feels in the way.
POINTED TIPS	Stubborn, efficient, conscientious.
WIDER AT TOP	A stimulating house for a cat to be in.
LARGE	Cat will demand attention and sympathy.
SMALL	A house worth hanging around.
THICK	Good sign for a cat.
THIN	Cat will be cared for well.

EARS OF CAT	
LARGE	Lively and demonstrative cat, often with placid owner.
SMALL	Cat sleeps a lot, owners on the go.
SHARP TIPS	Cats want their own way, become cunning and conniving because human can be slow to react to cat's needs.
ROUNDED EDGES	Owner is controlling, cat happy to be submissive and to wait for feeding.

LOBES

Lobes describe someone's love life. If she has large and thick lobes, a person is going to have good fortune and above average wealth. Her love life may not be all that rosy, but her cat will be well looked after, possibly taking the place of an opposite-sex partner.

Someone with small lobes has a strong sex drive, which means there will always be someone else in the house for a cat to harass when hungry. This owner has possible insecure relationships with her parents which may lead to emotional blocks later in life. There might be some competition for the cat's affections. She knows her cat is a source of relief and relaxation, and will come in for lots of heavy petting sessions. However, this does not necessarily make for closeness, much as a smothering mother may eventually drive a child away.

If the lobes are unusually tiny, it indicates a stubbornness and someone fond of material comforts. That usually includes having a cat around, but such an owner may overindulge and have time away from petting.

LOBES OF OWNER	
LARGE AND THICK	Cat ears the trousers!
SMALL LOBES	Cat will be petted a lot.
TINY LOBES	Petting is either feast or famine.

HAIR

Baldness means sensuousness and sensitivity. A cat will be well treated by someone losing or having lost a significant amount of their hair.

Thick hair indicates hard workers with varied goals. These people come home tired and don't want the cat sitting on their chair. Cat has to learn to share status.

A beard indicates trustworthiness in a person. But a bearded person does not trust others easily. Although he is honest, he is also careful. His cat rises in his estimation when it catches mice.

Those with sparse hair are said to exercise caution, not realising their true worth. They rely on the feedback of others to tell them of their successes. Cats in this household are proud and noble, and are apt to sprawl on beds, sofas and chairs despite often expressed opposition.

On a cat, whiskers are an excellent indicator of exploratory and hunting interests. At night, whiskers take the place of vision, detecting small changes in air pressure due to the nearby movements of small animals or insects. Those with the longer undamaged whiskers bite cleanly, whereas those cats whose whiskers are damaged misjudge the killing bite and can plunge its teeth into the wrong part of the prey's body.

HAIR OF OWNER	
BALDNESS	Cat well-liked.
BEARD	Cat is expected to earn her keep.
THICK	Good food, but cat might have to wait until human is ready.
SPARSE	Cats are king.

WHISKERS OF CAT	
LONG	Confident and content, owner though may have business worries.
DAMAGED	Cat stays in at night, wants entry to master bedroom. Owner often expresses annoyance.

WHAT IS YOUR BODY SAYING?

POSITIVE BODY LANGUAGE

Someone displaying positive body language will attract cats. The cats watch and wait to see:

* Relaxed posture
* Someone comfortably seated
* Not fidgeting, not jigging leg up and down.
* Relaxed breathing,
* No stiff, awkward or abrupt movements,
* Confident eyeball to eyeball contact,
* Looking away occasionally to avoid staring,
* Nodding agreement, leaning toward cat to speak,
* Uncrossed arms
* Hands open(palms turned upward)
* Smiling
* Animated gesturing.

If a cat sees any of the above it may feel confident about approaching a human, even a stranger

NEGATIVE BODY LANGUAGE

On the other hand, a person with negative body language

❖ Holds their body tense,
❖ Folds arms in front
❖ Has hands on or frequently touches her face
❖ Fidgets, can't keep still
❖ May have arms behind the head leaning back,
❖ Yawns a lot
❖ Displays outbursts of impatience,
❖ Leans away
❖ Nods her head in bird-like jerky movements.

Such a human is sending a 'keep away' message to a cat. Some cats will approach out of curiosity, but if so the movement will be guarded.

CATS ATTRACT HUMANS BY

❖ Lying on back with feet in the air
❖ Pawing and soft pummelling into lap
❖ Chinning human's leg
❖ Looking up and meowing

HOW DO YOU WALK?

F eet are a person's emotional foundation. How someone walks is supposed to be able to tell you much about how they handle the world, for instance what they are like in bed!

If they walk fast, it means they are generally impatient, lacking in passion. Such a person's cat will be passionate and will want more contact than the owner is prepared to give.

On the other hand, a slow walker gives herself time to smell the roses, enjoys walking and the side of life that is less concerned with monetary gain, and is more focussed on her quality of living. Consequently this owner will be one who is prepared to devote loving time to her cat.

Walking in a straight line means someone focussed, which eventually leads to good fortune. These people know what they want, are goal setters and have a fair idea as to how how they will be achieved. Their cat will be close by to reap the rewards of an abundant lifestyle.

The person who ambles from side to side is said to be a good lover, but is untidy. Small details like cleanliness are neglected, in favour of an enjoyment of life that borders on hedonism. A cat can come and go as she pleases in this house.

When the feet angle outwards, we say the person displays gluttony, selfishness, likes the good life, but nevertheless is successful. In this house the cat will always be asking for food, whining for tidbits and jumping on kitchen and table surfaces.

When the feet point inwards however, it indicates a person insecure, timid, and hesitant. In such a house the cat will be bold and try to take over.

WALK OF OWNER	
WALKS FAST	Cat may roam, looking for person with more warmth.
WALKS SLOWLY	Owner gives cat quality time.
STRAIGHT LINE	Cat won't go without for too long.
AMBLES SIDE-TO-SIDE	Cat can please itself.
FEET ANGLE OUTWARDS	Cat can sit on the dining table.
POINTING INWARDS	Cat thinks it is boss.

WALK OF CAT	
SURE-FOOTED	Cat is confident, intelligent, has an owner who doesn't walk much by choice.
STUMBLING GAIT	Owner may be interested in sport.
WALKS PROUDLY	Cat sociable, but owner shuns completely.
SLINKS	Could be other animals around, or noisy household.

HOW DOES YOUR HEAD MOVE?

During conversation, the head has three positions – straight up, cocked slightly on the side, or looking downwards. If someone's head is straight up, the person is said to be of 'neutral mind'. He/she will not be hurried. Their cat will be in a hurry though, and demand food exactly when she had it the previous day, and not a moment after.

A tilting head indicates interest, a desire to go to lower status to give the other person power. This person is self-conscious and a little apprehensive as a general stance in life. It is a protective device much like when a dog rolls over and exposes its underbelly. Such a person will tend to give her cat a lot of power, and the house may soon be revolving around the cat's needs.

Looking downward indicates desire to escape. It is a negative sign, the person is apt to be judgemental and someone who displays a slight hostility. This person's cat will stay near exits in case she has to leave in a hurry, as she finds the owner hard to get close to.

MOVEMENT OF THE OWNER'S HEAD	
STRAIGHT UP	Cat is impatient.
TILTING	Cat rules.
LOOKING DOWNWARDS	Cat stays close to cat door.

MOVEMENT OF THE CAT'S HEAD	
STRAIGHT AHEAD	Owner has little time for games.
LOOKS DOWN	Bowl not filled often enough.
LOOKS AROUND	Owner seen as relaxed and sociable.

HOW DO YOU SPEAK?

A person with a high pitched voice is visual, tidy, clean and neat. She will not enjoy dirt trailing in from the outside. Cat better watch herself because she herself is being watched as she goes either way through the door.

The low voiced owner is probably largely auditory and full of good humour. She is not as fussy as the high-voiced person, and she responds to flattery. There is nothing she likes better than hearing one of her children say to her I love you mummy. When the cat snuggles into her lap, she imagines that that is what the cat is saying.

A low, shaking voice is the kinaesthetic person, ruled by feelings, and liable to be fearful about life. She will respond best to a cat that is not too needy and appears to have its act together, the 'strong silent' type. She also is extremely sympathetic to a cat with a temporary disability, but not to one permanently too scarred.

An owner with a naturally soft voice can be insecure, waiting for others to speak first. She is reluctant to make decisions without someone else's approval and is also feelings-oriented. She will allow her cat to do what it likes before she decides how to respond.

The owner who speaks fast is easily offended but quick to forgive. She has concerns about money which dissipate if someone suggests a reason to spend more! This person is playful and encourages a cat to stay a kitten as long as it can get away with it.

A slow speaking person is fond of music and probably enjoys singing. She is sensual and loves matters of the occult. She sees herself as an earth mother and probably has a view or garden that she covets and shows to all visitors. Her cat is her secret pride and joy.

Sometimes a person can be heard to enunciate words as if they are Shakespearian actors. Teachers frequently speak thus; they have an appreciation for the spoken word and let each one out as if it was a precious gem. Such a person is careful in many other ways too. She has been let down more than once and is wary of relationships, yet she is caring, loyal and is a friend for life. But she suffers from bouts of melancholy, and longs for a spiritual twin or some deeper reason for her life. She very often lives alone and slightly away from the madding crowd. Her cat is very precious and can communicate with her without using words.

SPEECH OF OWNER	
HIGH PITCHED	Cat regarded as messy individual.
LOW VOICE	Owner will treat cat as one of her children.
LOW, SHAKING QUALITY	Cat will be brave but quite dependent.
LOUD VOICE	Quiet cat.
SOFT	Cat rules the roost.
FAST SPEECH	Cats can expect to be played with.
SLOW	Owner prefers dogs but tolerates cats if they don't misbehave.
DELIBERATE	Her cat is all she needs.

SPEECH OF CAT	
LOUD	Owner slow to respond to cat's wishes.
SOFT	Owner is assertive but matter-of-factual.
SHORT BURSTS	Owner pushes cat off surfaces even though cat was there first.
SUSTAINED	Owner keeps changing the rules.

WHAT'S IN A NAME?

Numerology is a very old science, some say the oldest and predates the holy scriptures by thousands of years. Numerologists believe that we are born on a certain date, hour and minute, not merely by chance, but in order to learn important lessons and perform certain tasks in the course of our lifetimes. At that time, presumably, the planets etc are in such and such position which make's one's destiny favourable.

It may equally be true that it operates in reverse – that mothers unknowingly give birth to their children on a particular date because on some subconscious level there is an underlying awareness that this date will serve an expectancy they might already have as to the personality of their unborn child.

Whether the chicken came first or the egg is always going to be debated. It can be argued that the egg uses the chicken to get another egg. The interesting truth is that numerology is studied by tens of thousands of people, and seems in many instances to be uncannily accurate. I can only say that of the people I know, and that includes my cat, it is bang on target.

I recently was taken around the country on a media tour to promote my last book *'Pawmistry-How To Read Your Cat's Paws'*(Penguin 1998). I appeared on TV and radio stations in many cities and towns, reading cats' paws. But I was actually using numerology to back my readings. Station managers would go home and get their cats, but before they did I would ask the cat's name. Then I would tell these owners roughly what type of cat they had. Many were amazed that I knew so much about an animal I had not yet met. How come?

What I believe happens is that owners give their cat names that are self-fulfilling expectancies of what they would like their cat to be. If you are a quiet owner, you will probably want a cat that makes interesting noises. Consequently you will probably give your cat a name that adds up to 3. Men seem to call their cats names that are macho, with hunter overtones. Names then occur like Bandit, Lothar and Zak, which add up to 1, 4, 5 or 8 – the numbers for the methodical execution of plans.

You will do this without ever realizing. The math of numbers runs through our veins and brains just as surely as it runs through a schoolbook. A wave breaks in a hyperbolic curve, as does a waterfall and the bullet from a gun. Planets are circles as are bubbles and certain atomic orbits. And a mathematical progression of numbers called the

Fibonacci Series, describes the way rabbits breed as well as the angle a leaf will make as it exits the stem of a plant. Aesthetics seem to be based on the math of nature outside of ourselves – Greek architecture utilises the Golden Ratio – which is exhibited on much of their architecture, and which again is related to the way the wave on the beach curls over.

It is not too fanciful then to assume that animals have this awareness. After all, bees and wasps can count up to a thousand, migratory birds use star grid patterns for navigation, and a starfish will be produced in a perfect star shape – with no math books or protractors to refer to on the ocean floor.

Perhaps what we call math is really only a tiny door opening into how nature operates. A cat may really analyse things numerically and without knowing it live up to its name simply because its owner reinforces what behaviours are expected.

GETTING THE VALUES

First, you find what the numerological value is for your name or birth date. All you do is add the letters of your name according to the table below:

1	2	3	4	5	6	7	8	9
A	B	C	D	E	F	G	H	I
J	K	L	M	N	O	P	Q	R
S	T	U	V	W	X	Y	Z	

So a name like Bandit will be 2+1+5+4+9+2 = 23, and 2+3=5. So Bandit would be called a '5', which is the number of the go-getter, or in cat-terms, a hunter. 5 is his 'Name Vibration'.

For a birth date, if say, Bandit was born on the 16th of the month, for example(1+6), he would be a 7. This is his 'Day Born Vibration'.

If he was born in 1997, these (1+9+9+7)add up to 26, which reduces down to 8. So 8 is the 'Year Born Vibration.

And if his actual birth date was 16/1/97, you add all these (1+6+1+9+7)to get his Life Path Vibration.

WORKING OUT A READING

So for our mythical subject 'Bandit' we have:
- ❖ WholeNameNumber (WN) =5 (Essence of his Being, his Destiny, or Basic Character)
- ❖ Name First Vowel (NF)=a=1(Inner self)
- ❖ ConsonantNumber (CN) = (b+n+d+t) = 4 (Outer Personality)
- ❖ Day Born Number (DB) = 7
- ❖ Year Born Number (YB) = 8
- ❖ Life Path Number (LP) = 8+7=6. (Career);

and from these we can do a reading such as this:

"Bandit is a natural hunter(WN=5). At times (YB=8) he is extremely successful, which he does alone and with great determination(NF=1). It is his main focus and he is a perfectionist(DB=7), always on the prowl inside and out for rodents. Everyone knows he is good(CN=4) He sees it as his job and responsibility(NF=1)and he feels the gratitude heaped on him by his owner. This creates a bond(6), and being a Capricorn(born in January)he has loyalty in very strong measure and the ability to manage his plans carefully(also reflected in 8). Bandit never brings bits of mouse inside because he is aware(LP=6) of home and harmony, which overrides everything else. Bandit's lesson to be learned is responsibility(6). In a previous life he was heartless and thoughtless and this resulted in him having to live on the streets. His career job now is to bring comfort and not to dominate the household by making those within too dependent on him, not easy to do because of his anxious desire to please."

NUMBERS AND MEANINGS OF CATS VS OWNERS

NUMBER 1: THE HEAD	
THE LONER; INFLUENTIAL	
QUALITIES OF A "1" OWNER	Action, ambition & leadership.
OPPOSING "1"	This cat will be non-affectionate, uncaring, and a loner.

NUMBER 2: THE EMOTIONS	
THE MANIPULATOR; NEEDS ASSURANCE	
QUALITIES OF A "2" OWNER	Balance, passivity and receptivity.
OPPOSING "2"	This cat will be non-affectionate, uncaring, and a loner.

NUMBER 3: ENERGY	
THE CHILD	
QUALITIES OF A "3" OWNER	Gaiety, versatility, joyous, brilliance.
OPPOSING "3"	This cat will be quiet and melancholic.

NUMBER 4: BALANCE	
THE WORKER	
QUALITIES OF A "4" OWNER	Endurance, steadiness and dullness.
OPPOSING "4"	This cat will be a free-spirit, careless and fickle.

NUMBER 5: VARIETY	
QUALITIES OF A "5" OWNER	Sexuality, adventure and instability.
OPPOSING "5"	This cat will be resentful of change, with low self-image.

NUMBER 6: CREATIVITY THE ARTIST	
QUALITIES OF A "6" OWNER	Domesticity, harmony, home and hearth, dependability.
OPPOSING "6"	This cat will be a roamer.

NUMBER 7: MYSTICAL THE PERFECTIONIST	
QUALITIES OF A "7" OWNER	Mysterious, knowledgeable, solitary.
OPPOSING "7"	This cat will be unthinking, less than fussy.

NUMBER 8: MATERIAL THE MANAGER; UNDEMONSTRATIVE	
QUALITIES OF A "8" OWNER	Worldly involvement, material success.
OPPOSING "8"	This cat will be ill-fated, a bad manager.

NUMBER 9: THE SPIRIT	
QUALITIES OF A "9" OWNER	Spirituality, inspiration and achievement.
OPPOSING "9"	This cat will be thick skinned, have no moral fibre, and be passive.

NUMEROLOGICAL COMPATIBILITIES

Compatibility between cats and owners can be determined by comparing Date of Birth Numbers. The following list has all the number combinations. Look up your own and compare it to that of your cat!

SCORING			
A	B	C	D
Amazing	Business-like	Cautious	Dismal

1 and 1	A	4 and 4	A
1 and 2	A	4 and 5	C
1 and 3	B	4 and 6	B
1 and 4	D	4 and 7	A
1 and 5	C	4 and 8	B
1 and 6	B	4 and 9	B
1 and 7	C		
1 and 8	A/D	5 and 5	A/D
1 and 9	A	5 and 6	B
		5 and 7	D
2 and 2	A	5 and 8	A
2 and 3	B	5 and 9	B
2 and 4	B		
2 and 5	D	6 and 6	A
2 and 6	B	6 and 7	D
2 and 7	B	6 and 8	A
2 and 8	B	6 and 9	A
2 and 9	A		
		7 and 7	A
3 and 3	A/D	7 and 8	B
3 and 4	C	7 and 9	A
3 and 5	C		
3 and 6	B	8 and 8	A
3 and 7	B	8 and 9	B
3 and 8	C		
3 and 9	A	9 and 9	A

WHAT STORY DO YOUR HANDS TELL?

R est your left hand loosely on a table, palm upwards. If there is quite a gap between the first two fingers – you have a talent for making decisions. On your cat, use the left paw turned upwards, and look at the gap between the first two digits(if she'll let you!)

If a gap between 3rd and 4th, this indicates a person or a cat has independence of action

DIGIT SEPARATION	
BETWEEN 1ST & 2ND	Decisive.
BETWEEN 2ND & 3RD	Independent thinker.
BETWEEN 3RD & 4TH	Independent of action - a hidden and unusual relationship already with someone, or an unconventional thinker about sex and relationships

HAND SHAPE	
LONG	Sensitive, musical or artistic, detail, expressive.
SMALL	Much energy.
KNOBBLY JOINTS	One who loves to argue.

FEEL OF HAND	
SMOOTH	Those who don't like to debate and argue.
HARD	Energy and perseverance.
SOFT	Laziness of mind and body.

SKIN	
SOFT	Impressionable.
HARD	Quarrelsome.

NAILS/CLAWS	
LARGE	Successful in business.
SHORT	High blood pressure, heart complaints, criticism and contradiction.
WIDER THAN LONG	Obstinacy.
THIN, RIDGED, HARD	Delicate health.

LINES	
DEEP	Controlling person or cat.
SHALLOW	One pushed around by others.

IF A CAT/HUMAN RELATIONSHIP IS TO LAST...

People always want to know if they are compatible with their pets. It is possible to use palmistry and pawmistry to determine this. Look at the Heart Lines on the left hands of each of you (owner and cat).

A sign of compatibility is if the heart lines on both individuals are similar. Look at your cat's left paw and your own left hand. Hold your hand so the fingers are pointing horizontally. Your heart line is on the right. On your cat the heart line is the right line of the two lines that divide the large pad into three segments.

If the Heart Line (nearest fingers) is curved – you are masculine, have a physical approach to sex, are aggressive in love, demonstrative in affection and have a more emotional approach to relationships. You are the one who starts new relationships rather than waiting for them to begin; the one who looks for warmth, love and affection in sex, and the one who shows feelings clearly and demonstratively and in this relationship at least, takes the lead. You don't usually date anyone who is plain looking and you are prepared to do all the courting and seduction.

If the Heart Line is straight – this indicates a feminine or mental attitude and describes one is receptive in love, who talks and thinks about it more than does anything, has a cool thoughtful approach, finds relationships develop by themselves; looks for compatibility, affection and companionship in sex; and would rather share responsibility in a relationship rather than wanting to be the dominant partner. This person would consider a plain person. The straight-heart-lined are the ones who are courted and seduced.

If your straight line comes across and ends up under the second finger, than you have a stronger sex drive than the desire for feeling and warmth.

When the line is straight and short – this indicates a crude sex drive, not much thoughtfulness, and not much sensitivity.

Look on your left hand with the fingers pointing upward. If the heart line droops downward on the right, you can be hurt very easily in love.

LENGTH OF HUMAN FINGERS	
LONG TOP JOINTS	Thoughtful, religious.
LONG MIDDLE JOINTS	Skillful in business.
LONG BOTTOM JOINTS	Greedy, self-indulgent.

1ST FINGER (HUMAN)	
SHOWS	Self-confidence.
SYMBOL	Of the self.
IF LONG	Bossy, self-aware, self-confident, could be a priest, aware of own abilities, interested in self-

	development and advancement. Keen to have things his/her own way. Possibly bossy or conceited, able to take charge.
IF SHORT	Shy, afraid of failure, inclined to self-doubt and self-criticism.
IF FINGER HELD JUTTING OUTWARDS	Probably overacts to compensate and so appears aggressive and independent.
IF CURVED	Great need for security, therefore have many hobbies and collect many possessions, may be stamp and coin collectors.
TOP PHALANGE LONG	Philosophical, theories.
MIDDLE LONG	Ambitious.
BOTTOM LONG	Wants to rule over others.

2ND FINGER (HUMAN)	
SHOWS	Serious side of the personality, business talent, reliability, steadiness.
SYMBOL	Of seriousness.
IF LONG	Person treats life seriously, believes in getting ahead and being successful. Business people who deal with money and property.
IF SHORT & STUBBY	Careless, don't like to hold a responsible job. Hippies and dropouts.
TOP PHALANGE LONG	Melancholy.
MIDDLE LONG	Good in business, loves plants and nature.
BOTTOM LONG	Collector, won't throw anything away.

3ʳᵈ FINGER (HUMAN)	
SHOWS	Creativity and artistic qualities, talent for drawing and designing.
IF LONG	Creative nature, artist.
IF SHORT	Short ring fingers are very rare.
TOP PHALANGE LONG	Love of colour.
MIDDLE LONG	Love of work.
BOTTOM LONG	Love of display, vanity, showing off, riches.

4ᵗʰ FINGER (HUMAN)	
SHOWS	Sex and communication.
IF LONG	Ability to write or speak, also strong sex drive and above average intelligence.
IF SHORT	Immaturity in emotional and sexual behaviour, childlike, playful, joyful and always fresh.
IF LOW-SET	Some childhood difficulty connected with a parent has affected the person's emotional outlook.
IF STICKING OUT	Temporary emotional or social difficulties with spouse, could mean loss of loved one.
TOP PHALANGE LONG	Love of talking.
MIDDLE LONG	Industrious, common-sense, likes to argue.
MIDDLE SHORT	Completely disorganised.
BOTTOM LONG	Scheming, lying.

❖ If little finger swollen at the top – person loves writing.

❖ If it doesn't extend past middle phalange of ring finger – person is ruled by others.

❖ If ring finger and middle finger bend toward each other – sacrifices are continually being made.

❖ If little finger curves toward the middle finger – a shrewd mind, person almost dishonest.

What is your motivational Drive?

Everyone is said to be born with 4 basic motivational drives. With these in place we can achieve whatever goals we set out for. Those with their drives are:

1. THE AUTHORITY SEEKER
   Is powerful, choleric & dominant.

2. THE ATTENTION SEEKER
   Is popular, friendly & affectionate.

3. THE AGREEMENT SEEKER
   Is peaceable, balanced, stable, and likes the status quo.

4. THE ACCURACY SEEKER
   Is easily frustrated, analytical, cautious, has disciplinarian tendencies, and seeks perfection.

AUTHORITY SEEKERS

Do-ers, confident, bossy, loud, blunt, know-alls, learn by doing, must have own way, forthright, correct others, less caring, take risks.

ATTENTION SEEKERS

Playful, joking, learn by talking, enjoy stories, love dressing up, born actors, tend to wander, volunteer for high profile things that might earn praise, must be loved, need company.

AGREEMENT SEEKERS

Learn by watching from a safe distance, stable, quiet, introverted, hate attention, indecisive, nervous about change, friendly to everyone, in rut, consistent, courteous, obedient, sharing, like reading

ACCURACY SEEKERS

Sarcastic, cold, insist on being right, academic, pessimistic, loners, learn by thinking, frown most of the time, serious, neat, disciplined

Those who do not see cats as agreement seekers and attention seekers view them as stereotypes. That is, they invariably think cats are all the same because these two types love company, whine and talk on and on meaninglessly. To a certain extent then it is a true observation. But live with a cat day in and day out and you'll see more sides to him!

If we plot the four thus:

ACCURACY SEEKER	AUTHORITY SEEKER
AGREEMENT SEEKER	ATTENTION SEEKER

We note that neighbouring categories up or across (e.g. agreement + attention, accuracy + agreement) have the strongest relationship, whereas diagonally opposing categories (e.g. agreement + authority) don't get on at all well.

WHAT MOTIVATES CATS

The Authority Seeking Cat
Takes risks on high ledges and in stealing food from the table, grabs the best sofa before the human does, knocks over ornaments and doesn't bother to run away, demands food when hungry, wakes owners in the middle of the night if wants to be let out.

The Attention Seeking Cat
Sits by the door or window where he will be easily seen, lays or sprawls on floor so he will be noticed,

talks and purrs a lot, knocks things over and runs under the bed then peaks out to see if he is being chased, jumps in laps and cajoles humans to stroke him.

The Agreement Seeking Cat

Sees himself as part of a team household with each having his place, sits in unobtrusive spots, plays safe at all times, jumps up if human wants to sit down, brings other cats home to share his food bowl, grooms himself incessantly, holds old grudges, not necessarily a very good hunter – may be too slow to act. This is universally the best cat to have around.

The Accuracy Seeking Cat

Can plan and attack fairly large birds and other cats or dogs who threaten territory, makes nest area away from hustle and bustle of main house, is scrupulously clean and upset if litter-box not cleaned regularly, is insistent about meals on time and that owner returns home at the same time each day like clockwork

DRIVES COMPATIBILITIES

Whatever you and your cat decide you are, will determine how well you get on together. Two Attention Seekers will get on just fine, as will two Agreement Seekers.

Agreement and Accuracy Seekers will be a good combination too, because one wants direction and the other offers it. One is happy being high status and the other is content with low status.

Two Accuracy seekers succeed together well because of mutual respect. Each has a bottom line which is displayed when the other crosses it.

When both of you are Authority seekers, you each need plenty of space and opportunity to do your own thing without affecting the other. Both want to be the boss. There must be a silent agreement that each has his own area of expertise.

Authority and Attention seekers can get on if the Attention seeker decides the concessions are worth it. The attention seeker is therefore really in charge.

In the case of Attention and Agreement Seekers, both value communication and company and can co-inhabit very well. Once again, the Attention seeker is in control.

If one is an Attention seeker and the other an Accuracy seeker, things may not always be harmonious. The Accuracy seeker must be prepared to swallow pride and forgive.

When it comes to the Agreement seeker and the Authority seeker, one seeks leadership and the other desires to be led. The Agreement Seeker is in control and the relationship is as successful as the concessions and tolerances of the situation are.

What about Accuracy and Authority Seekers? This would not work between a cat and a human. One would have to change. If you acquire a cat from another home and it finds itself in this scenario, it will either run away or adapt by changing itself into another motivational mode.

Accuracy and Attention Seekers are similarly doomed. One seeks noise and the other wants peace and quiet.

PERSONALITY, TEMPERAMENT AND CHARACTER

JUST WHAT IS A PERSONALITY?

Cats have personalities, just like people. Your cat is different from the cat next door and in any litter there will be one that stands out as being more active and alert, one more sleepy and perhaps one appearing timid. Just as psychology is the study of behaviour, personality is the study of individual behaviour.

There is no such thing as a good or a bad personality. Every human being and cat has his or her personal strength.

The scope of study is vast; in humans covering genetic predisposition, experience as children to develop behavioural consistencies over a life span, emotional reactions, and whatever can be plotted to predict job outcomes and lifetime satisfaction.

It is the same for cats – whatever is seen as the kitten 'type' will most likely persist throughout later cat life. Every member of every species needs to meet the challenges of survival and of reproduction. How these challenges are met within a species reflects species-typical solutions. Understanding how these problems are answered by humans enables us to understand the fundamentals of human nature. As humans are animals and cats are also animals, what we call human nature is not too far removed from what is cat-nature.

The past few years have seen a resurgence of interest in personality. Research spanning the range from genes to the life-span, from the individual to the species, and from the normal to the pathological is being carried out in the name of personality theory. What is integrating much of this work is an emphasis not just on description, but on the functions that personality serves.

Perhaps the most important is the phenomenon of two individuals that share the same environment, for whatever was brought to the situation before on the part of each contributor, now gets modified and adapted to the other, which provides much mutual interest and fascination for each. This applies equally to people and people, cats and people, and cats and other cats.

PERSONALITIES OF CATS

Cats regard us in one of three ways: as litter mates, as dependents, or as they might have done. Nervous, unsettled behaviour will be typical of cats who are either timid and fearful of people *or* overly dependent on them.

Consequently, cats grow up with fixed personalities, some dependent, some very sociable, some angry and some emotionally handicapped. That means they will feel more comfortable cohabiting in homes with the personalities of people which suit them, and accordingly they tend to gravitate toward those environments.

WHAT IS *YOUR* PERSONALITY?

Do you have a guiding motto, a message that seems to sum you up? We can determine your personality type, then we can see the kind of cat that probably would attach itself to you, above others. Then we can work backwards, for looking at how your cat behaves with you tells you what sort of personality you *really* have.

If you are game for an experiment, ask yourself is there any one sentence in the list below that you feel you can internally relate to, more than any other?

1. THE REFORMER/CRITIC	
PEOPLE WHO SAY:	"I do everything the right way. Everyone else is wrong."
CATEGORIES	Idealists, Perfectionists, Controllers.

2. THE HELPER	
PEOPLE WHO SAY:	"I must help others. They need me."
CATEGORIES	Flirt, Seductive, Healer.

3. THE MOTIVATOR	
PEOPLE WHO SAY:	"I need to succeed. People are watching."
CATEGORIES	Neurotic, Fearful, Social.

4. THE DRAMATIC/ROMANTIC	
PEOPLE WHO SAY:	"I am unique."
CATEGORIES	Long-suffering.

5. THE THINKERS	
PEOPLE WHO SAY:	"I need to understand the world. I must sort myself out."
CATEGORIES	Melancholic, Thoughtful, Lonely.

6. THE COUNTER-PHOBICS	
PEOPLE WHO SAY:	"I am affectionate and skeptical."
CATEGORIES	Negative Expectations.

7. THE SUNNY ENTHUSIASTS	
PEOPLE WHO SAY:	"I am happy and open to new things."
CATEGORIES	Cheerful, Optimistic.

8. THE SUPER LEADERS	
PEOPLE WHO SAY:	"I must be strong."
CATEGORIES	Assertive.

9. THE INSTINCTIVE PEACEMAKERS	
PEOPLE WHO SAY:	"I am at peace. I go with the flow."
CATEGORIES	Intelligent.

Remember your number. We will now use that to try to describe you a little more fully.

ONES

Idealists

Idealists devote themselves to cultivating inner purity. They turn their energies outward to investigate the public world and to develop and spread social awareness. They have a fervent desire to spread the news of their experience of what they consider to be good and evil. Idealists are interested in understanding the significance of things; inventing theories for what they think life is about. Rather than just taking people as they find them, they nurture the ethical and moralistic.

They are highly romantic in their interpretation of the real world, seeing high drama in their quest for life, and have an irresistible urge to enlighten others. Idealists can quite easily strain their relationships by reading too much into some hidden meanings in their loved ones' words. While their heads are clear, often their houses and grounds are untidy and look neglected. But this suits a cat, because nooks and crannies abound.

But all their cats want is a quiet life, with no fuss or fanfare. Whereas their owners get carried away with the rightness of their position and find themselves preaching to friends to convince them of their point of view, their cats are mainly silent and shy, doing everything with trepidation.

Cats are very attracted to idealists. For this reason, many philosophers have cats, and mutual respect flows because each understands the other.

Perfectionists

These people grew up in an atmosphere in which they were criticised, perhaps severely and were told that criticism was done in the name of love. As a child they were told *'If I didn't love you, I wouldn't correct you. I tell you what is wrong because I love you.'* They look at society and see only what is wrong, sorting for fault, for flaws, or for what ought to be there and isn't. They have high standards to which reality must, but cannot, conform. Consequently they turn the scolding light of fault-finding on themselves first, and to be good to themselves, they are self-critical. Implicit in this approach is a smouldering anger that things are not right. They can be pictured as waving their index finger in a scolding manner.

They will work endlessly on a project, making sure everything is perfect, and they frequently have trouble with deadlines because almost any project can be improved .

They have cats that tend to give up easily and walk away from difficult situations. These cats seem to have no moral concern and act as if they couldn't care less. Perfectionists see their life's work as reforming those they love. For possibly this reason, many marry alcoholics or spouses addicted to something, like work or sport, only to become polarised against their own sensuality because sensuality can easily lead to moral deviance.

Passion, impulse, bliss — these threaten the moral order of the Perfectionist. Hence they do not indulge, overeat, or act impulsively. Unlike their cats!

If you see a very fat, easy-going, placid cat, it probably lives with a perfectionist. It may go through periods when it urinates on the carpet, defecates in the hall and scratches the wrong surfaces. In short, enjoying doing naughty things to gain attention.

Controllers

Some people live in a hostile world and are fiercely loyal to those they love and want to protect. They look for power in all situations. In a hostile world you have to know who is powerful and who isn't. Many will start fights, verbal or physical, just to find out the strength of their partner. If you stand strong in one way or another, you earn this person's respect. If you are weak, no amount of goodness or placating or appeal to authority will endear you to them.

These are people who probably prefer dogs anyway, are fiercely loyal, especially in combat, so they make fine teammates And in combat too, another characteristic shows up: they frequently have extremely high pain thresholds. They pride themselves on not showing or giving into weakness or pain and focus their attention outwardly.

They like their power physical, not mental or artistic, so football suits them well. Football teams often foster fierce rivalries. People who oppose these folk can become objects of obsessive hatred. They are also ultra-responsible at times, and can become unreasonable, making exorbitant demands on their body or driving themselves to get control of a situation, a business or a relationship.

Controllers feel they are number one and inflate their presence, filling up a room with their expansive energy. This expansion is in service of protecting the soft inner self within. You would be wise to approach such a person with gentleness. Many women with husbands of this type describe them as pussy-cats, but they are the only ones that get to see this person's soft underbelly. Beneath that bluff exterior is a child in need of protection.

Tears are never too far away, as they are super-conscious of fairness. One reason they are hostile is that they see the world as hostile and unfair. When they are entranced they seek vengeance instead of justice, but when healthy they appreciate justice a great deal. Sometimes they see themselves as having to defend themselves against a system rigged against them. Giving up one's body for the team is considered a highly virtuous act. But they often cannot hear opposition. Nuance is important to the Controlling Personality.

But in this house, surprisingly, the cat often rules. This comes about because a Controller sees home as another team situation, led by the member who most prides its independence. It will always be the cat.

TWOS

The Flirt/Seductive

They emotionally invest in others by helping. The flirt/seductive has unconscious hostility, even hatred, for whoever is their 'target' person and is invariably disappointed as this is rooted in fatherlessness, actual or perceived. A distant or frequently absent father who then periodically showers inappropriate attention on the little girl can create the lifelong message 'Either I'm totally lovable or I'm overlooked.' This gives a life-message to the little girl to work hard to please men.

But later, men may take her signals the wrong way, which infuriates her and so she moves to vengeance. Often reference is made to a man's duty to be responsible and take care of his obligations. His duty always includes taking care of her. She is functionally a child, and, according to her expectancy, his responsibility.

Flirt/seductives oscillate between intimacy and distance, using sexuality without emotional context. This makes it more passionate and less dependable. The cat will be stroked passionately one minute and ignored the next.

Boundaries are a problem for the flirt/seductive, and they will invite more intimacy than is appropriate. They might encourage someone to take advantage, sexually or financially. It is common that they dress to flirt; very short tight skirts if a woman and opened front shirts if a man. Really, they see themselves as having no power, yet exercising considerable power. She might see herself as nothing without the man, while at the same time scorning him. Yet she seldom has a life independent of the man, whose responsibility is in direct proportion to her need.

Because seduction is a way of life, she includes Divine Love in the same dynamic. These people are do-gooders who imagine that if they are Mother Theresas, so good and so loving, then they will be loved in return. Every community is apt to have a few of these whose 'invested' love is feared by many.

A cat here will be expected to 'provide' – in rodent extermination, prizes at cat shows or in affection at the owner's beck and call. A cat in this household will not be manipulative of the owner. There is no need to be. The owner will be doing all she can to 'buy' the cat's love. Either this cat's relationship with its owner is fantastic or it will be disastrous. Cats are wise enough to feel what is going on and largely try to stay away. They will not be controlled.

Flirt/seductives often prefer dogs, whom they can feel more power over.

Healers

Healers are found in only 1 percent of the general population, although, at times, their idealism leaves them feeling even more isolated from the rest of humanity.

They care passionately about a few special persons or a favourite cause, and their aim is to bring peace and integrity to their loved ones and the world. Their efforts are boundless and selfless, inspiring them to make extraordinary sacrifices for what they believe in.

Healers seek unity of body and mind, and of emotions and intellect, because most have a sense of inner division which comes from an unhappy upbringing. Healers grow up a fantasy-filled childhood, which is discouraged or even punished by their parents. From practical-minded families, they are often required by their parents to be sociable and industrious and they invariably have down-to-earth siblings who conform more to parental expectations.

They come to see themselves as misfits. Wishing to please their parents and siblings, but not knowing quite how, they wonder whether they are OK. They are like swans reared in a family of ducks. Deeply committed to the positive and the good, some develop a fascination with the problem of good and evil, sacred and profane.

When they believe they have dropped their guard and yielded to an impure temptation, they may be given to acts of self-sacrifice in atonement. Others seldom detect this inner turmoil, however, for the struggle between good and evil is within the person herself, and she does not feel compelled to make the issue public.

This person's cat is likely to be the sort of animal who will allow itself to be picked up or stroked by anyone. When it comes to the crunch though, it may be non-co-operative and refuse to come when called, even though it is hungry. Its feet are firmly on the ground and at first glance this cat often seems troubled while at the same time outgoing. The bold friendly look is sometimes a ploy for food and nothing more: on the inside this cat is anything but brave. It knows it will be fed, usually overfed by its caring and worrying owner, which affords the development of a capacity for silent indifference not always found in other cats.

THREES

Neurotic

The neurotic category is generally not one we would give to ourselves. But someone you know may fit this description. These are people who are in the image-confusion centre, rating themselves as to how others rate them. They tend to have cats who are very self-confident and spiritual, letting the world go by quietly and without fuss. These cats are seldom vocal but when they want something they act quickly, before anyone has the chance to stop them.

Although their emotionally charged owners can be very nice, it is usually somewhat of an act. The serenity in their cats though, is real. These are cats who command respect and refuse to eat what does not please them.

When free to choose situations, individuals sensitive to negative affect (neurotics) will try to avoid anything threatening. On the other hand, cats of neurotics take risks. It is always the emotionally stable individual who is more likely to participate voluntarily in activities that potentially result in negative affect.

Neurotic people are extremely sensitive to the needs and wants of others - their emotional life depends on them, In healthy people this becomes nurturing friendship, but in the neurotic it can become devouring invasiveness, complete co-dependency, and much flattery or seduction. If you see a matter of fact cat that makes no emotional demands, yet appears confident and secure, chances are that its owner will be neurotic.

Fearful

There are some humans for whom irrational fear is a basic preoccupation. They live in varying degrees of terror, partially because they live from their 'head' centre. They think a lot and frighten themselves. In their will is some sort of self-imposed knot and they have a variety of ways of not being able to take action. These two characteristics, fear and thinking, come together via anticipation. Some expect to run out of resources, so they frequently, (especially under stress) hoard time, energy and money.

Expecting the worst to happen, they spend a lot of time making sure they are protected against every eventuality. They don't expect things to work out very well, so they have multiple options and seldom excel in any one thing.

Fear-based people have cats that take on impossible challenges. These cats may be found up very tall trees, try to hunt prey or take on adversaries larger than themselves. Although they possess a quiet courage, they may occasionally hurl themselves into battle or think nothing of standing erect on their hind legs hammering their front paws on the back door demanding to be let in.

Social

These emotionally invest in others by performing for them. Outgoing and accomplished, the Social person is valued for what she can do and what kind of image she creates. Because she already has an inner belief that she is a loser, the slightest loss confirms this world-view She enjoys achievement, glory and the exertion, but losing hits hard. The only time she feels she can rest is the brief period after winning. She is liable to be are cocky, materialistic and talk of continually trying harder. Often she will shut her emotions down to get the job done.

Careful score keeping is this person's burden and the source of much compulsive energy. In the western world money is not for greed, or security or luxury, but to keep score.

Competition is supposed to bring out the best, to give us self-esteem, but in reality it undermines it. Competition is an addiction that is infinite. Unless she wins all the time, the Social slips into antisocial - the inward image of a loser. Any defeat gets internalised into despair.

She needs to excel, to achieve success, prestige, or recognition in any form, to achieve a feeling of the type of strength that comes from acclaim and supremacy. In one sense she is totally dependent on being observed.

Cats of these owners do not look for contests. They know they can go the highest, for the longest, and catch the biggest and the best. Knowing that removes the necessity to prove it. They are conscious of their own territory, and will pick owners who are friendly and neighbourly.

The more friendly you are with your neighbours, and the more you visit one another and go into each other's gardens, then the more tolerant the cats in each household will need to be of each other. That is not to say that each respective cat will freely go next door. Tolerance goes both ways, and in this case the opposite applies; each cat respecting that the domain of each is for exclusive use of the resident only. There is no need to continually test the waters.

FOURS

The Long Suffering

This person typically feels defective, unlovable and abandoned, rejecting people before they can reject her. She also tends to be enormously influenced by others. She lacks a certain inner density so that she is not sure of who she is. She pays too much attention to what others think of her and has a negative relationship to those around her. She takes pride in being different, especially being defective.

All the while lamenting her lot in life, you can hear a faint bragging as if she has been singled out by fate to suffer. Nobody knows the trouble she's seen, and nobody appreciates how she has handled it.

One payoff comes in the speech pattern of lamentation. The drama's the thing and envy is really her ticket to esteem. She expects esteem from others precisely because of her suffering. This also frequently creates a disdain for the ordinary, coupled with a vivid inner life. Her inner feelings are to the fore.

She may have a tendency to compare what is with what is missing and then spend a lot of emotional energy lamenting absence.

Her cat will be absent most of the time (a typical snare – something to fret over). This cat will decide to spend time where conditions are less theatrical and less highly charged. Not a vocal cat, wanting a contented life, it is rather detached from anything passionate. It does not brood about its inner life. This cat's owner often rejects others in the name of feeling rejected by them. One thing she can and should do is to make sure she gets plenty of physical exercise. It puts one in better contact with external reality. And her cat needs to come home.

FIVES

Melancholy

If you are a melancholy person, you appear sullen and introverted, and the chances are that you will find yourself with an alert, breezy cat, rather vocal and playful. If you are this sad person and find yourself drawn to a quiet little kitten, which you decide to take home because of its mournful little eyes, one of you will soon undergo change.

If it is the kitten that undergoes the transformation, and it grows into a cat with a sunny disposition, it may retain its timidity amongst other cats and possibly be victimised, thus forcing it indoors for much of the time. Such a cat will not be interested in venturing out at night.

But if *you* change, your previous sadness being but of a temporary nature, and the cat retains its quiet gloominess, it will be forever aloof and suspicious of anyone who comes to the house, making itself scarce at the sound of strange voices.

Thoughtful

A thoughtful person, one who spends much time in studious contemplation, will have a cat who is territorial, sitting on the doorstep or at the top of the drive for most of the day, surveying all who would enter. This cat is more interested in preventing other animals from hunting on its turf than doing any real hunting itself.

They see people as draining them, after which they are recharged by solitude These are extremely emotionally sensitive, often hypersensitive. So to protect this sensitivity, they develop unusually strong boundaries which include detachment. Non-involvement, being just an observer, is one way of insuring that one is not invaded.   There is a specific fear of being overwhelmed. Their island is protected by distance, not by hostility or placation.

The Lonely are also the most intellectual. Many are excellent writers because they are keen observers, they can replay and rehearse, make minute analyses and relate what they saw. While they are distant, they are also objective. They don't allow emotion to cloud their judgement, being not involved.

People are attracted to the lonely because of their sensitivity and intelligence. However, lonely people often require a long time to process material. They hate surprises and love privacy. Rather than hoarding money, they hoard emotions, time and personal giving of time and energy.

The Cat in this house will be very social. The people will be regarded as an asset rather than a liability. The cat is spoken about as one who forgives immediately, holds no grudges, is a 'people cat.' The cat is more involved with you than you are with it. It just won't keep its distance. The cat in this house feels that its life is enriched by its owner.

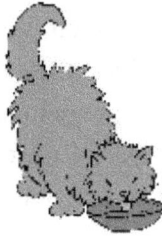

SIXES

Negative Expectations

This is an person with a lively ambiance and a wonderful loyalty to her family, even after they have been abusive.. Her fears feed her psyche. Fear, to this person, is the very reason for any action, rather than a reason to abstain.

Mostly, these fears are not about real things. *Real* crises are often handled quite well. Whatever can go wrong, in this person's imagination, will go wrong, and it's going to be worse than anyone can possibly imagine. In fact they go looking for what can go wrong. They interpret everything in the light of the danger they imagine is there.

The Cat in this environment relates mainly to one individual, but won't whine in neediness. It is aloof, detached, and considered cold and calculating. Often pushed out the door and told to earn its keep, it is seen as a lazy individual and a free-loader. But this is a cat quietly effective in the outside world, and knows about precision of movement. It is afraid of real dangers, not imagined. That's why it is constantly up trees and on narrow perches. It goes looking for excitement and success. It is not afraid but when real danger comes, it calculates first, rather than acting impulsively.

SEVENS

Cheerful and Optimistic

These are high energy, multi-interest people who see what they want to see, often through rose-coloured spectacles. They tend to live in the future (when they are sure their current plans will bring them happiness). 'We're in a bad patch just now, but things will get better' They have backup plans and use their head to create happiness.

Their chief tool is rationalization. If an event occurs in their life, others might call it bad, but they readjust their way of looking at it until they can see the bright side. One sign is unbounded energy; climbing mountains, bungy-jumping, travel, dancing and making friends in high places. These are telltale signs of a search for expansive experiences.

They feel inwardly trapped - this is their polarization, and because of this inner confinement, even suffocation at times, so they love heights, movement and high energy activities. Many are highly creative and innovative, rather susceptible to the lure of novelty.

If a man, he is probably gadget-crazy; if a woman she may have a high turnover in friends or relationships. Their low-stress coping style of looking at the high side of things and their mental mischief, tend to be easy on the body, so they live long. When you see old folks skydiving or climbing mountains, you'll know they are this type.

Often only they, according to them, are right and everybody else is wrong. Their enthusiasm is infectious and many flock to be in their presence. These folk dissociate from negative experiences. This works well in the short run because they experience mostly good things. Because they are unable to learn much or profit much from painful experiences, they don't mature. It's more fun to stay a child.

Their cats tend to be slow and heavy, with a wisdom that seems quite uncanny. These are not cats that take risks. The behaviour of their owners often mystifies them, because things keep changing; for instance the food bowl appears in different places. Because there tends to be noise in the house, these cats go outside for some peace and quiet. They seem less tolerant, aloof and less playful than other cats.

EIGHTS

Assertive

Perhaps you assign yourself an assertive personality. If so, you would typically spend much time outdoors, possibly gardening or paying attention to house tidiness and appearance. A cat in this environment often finds hunting rather difficult, as others are always interrupting its domain. Such a cat either roams widely in search of wilder safaris, or, if a large cat, stays in the house all day every day, watching those outside from the safety of the sill.

NINES

Intelligent

Intelligent folk are brimming with ideas, yet often with no priorities. Sometimes they are called drifters or chameleons; blowing whichever way the wind is blowing. Their loyalties are thin and temporary.

They make good politicians, because they can be insincere and smooth talkers with one real objective: to make themselves look good. They also make good sportsmen, because they can be intensely focussed for short periods of time.

But in a strange way some often don't think clearly, especially with words. They often have uncanny intuition - a "gut feeling" but they tend not to be articulate. Often these people find themselves in leadership roles because they know what everybody else wants and that is what they want.

They have wimpy cats that seem to go all out to make themselves unlovable and disrespected, even by people they depend on. They make themselves easy to attack. From kittenhood they perfected the art of getting stuck up trees, of straying into hostile environments. Where their owners just emotionally and intellectually just hunker down and lie low, they will cry pathetically if necessary.

Intelligent humans display a sweet quality about them with no hard edges. They have anger - a lot of it - but it's imploded, turned in on themselves. It smoulders, but it doesn't explode very often. Rather it becomes passive aggressive - extremely hard to deal with. Deep down they don't like conflict and would really like to co-operate.

But their cats complain bitterly at the slightest little grievance. They know what they would really like to do, but cannot decide how. They will sit blinking and staring at a bird hopping by them, not attacking simply because they are still deciding whether or not to do it.

However, these cats are loyal and trusting. All the high dramas are an act. Consequently, they often become the target of cruel children who throw them over balconies etc. These cats expect their meals on demand, not tied to some clock system. They tend to be quiet rather than vocal.

THE FOUR TEMPERAMENTS

Temperament has been likened to pre-disposition. For example, cats are predisposed - born - to hunt alone in the dark. Each cat, unless stopped in its maturation by an unfavourable environment, practices the habit or ability appropriate to this predisposition.

Put another way, our brain is a sort of computer which has temperament for its hardware and character for its software. The hardware is the physical base from which character emerges, placing an identifiable fingerprint on each individual's attitudes and actions.

This underlying consistency can be observed from a very early age, long before individual experience or social context has had time or occasion to imprint the person. Temperament is the word given to the inborn form of cat and human nature.

There are basically four temperaments*:

GUARDIANS	Ones & Eights	Idealists Perfectionists Controllers Assertives.
ARTISANS	Threes & Fours	Neurotic Fearful Social Long-suffering.
IDEALISTS	Twos & Sevens	Flirt/seductives Healers Cheerful Optimistic
RATIONALS	Fives & Nines	Melancholy Thoughtful Lonely Intelligent

GUARDIANS

Supervisors, Inspectors, Providers and Protectors.
They base their self-image on reliability, service, and respectability. Observing their close surroundings with a keen eye, they schedule their own and others'

activities so that needs are met and conduct is kept within bounds. Everything should be in its proper place, everybody should be doing what they're supposed to, everybody should be getting their just desserts, every action should be closely supervised, all products thoroughly inspected, all legitimate needs promptly met, all approved ventures carefully insured.

Though they might differ in being tough-minded or friendly in observing these schedules, and though they can be expressive or reserved in social attitude, all of them demand that ways and means of getting things done are proper and acceptable, according to *them*.

KEY WORDS FOR GUARDIANS	KEY WORDS FOR HIS CAT
Conservative	Wants a quiet life
Stable	Timid
Consistent	Changeable
Wants Routines	Doesn't push his luck
Sensible	Erratic
Factual	Illogical
Predictable	Unreliable
Patient	Impatient
Dependable	In world of its own
Hard-working	Often lazy
Detailed	Doesn't plan anything
Painstaking	Roughshod
Persevering	Gives up quickly
Thorough	Seems to do bare minimum

ARTISANS

Promoters, Crafters, Performers and Composers.

Arty types and do-ers who base their self-image on graceful action, bold spirit, and adaptability to circumstance. They probe around their immediate surroundings to detect and exploit any favourable options that came within reach. Having the freedom to act on the spur of the moment is very important to them. Everything is checked out for advantage.

Though they may differ in their attitude toward tough-mindedness and friendliness in exploring for options, and though some are socially expressive and some reserved, all are practical and effective in getting what they want.

KEY WORDS FOR ARTISANS	KEY WORDS FOR HIS CAT
Adaptable	Fixed
Artistic	Practical
Athletic	Moves only when necessary
Aware of, but not fighting, reality	Hangs back
Open-minded	Restricted
Seeks workable compromises	Seeks to slow life down
Know what happens around them	Is unaware of manipulation
Can see needs of moment	Slow to suss what's required
Stores up useful facts	Holds no grudges
Has no use for theories	Takes it one day at a time
Easy-going	Can be a stick-in-the-mud
Tolerant	Picky
Unprejudiced	Has decided who he likes
Persuasive	Not very vocal
Gifted with machines and tools	Clumsy hunter
Acts with effortless economy	Hangs back, waits too long
Sensitive to colour, line & texture	Insensitive to many things
Wants first-hand experiences	Content to watch others move
Enjoys life	Finds life a bit monotonous

IDEALISTS

Teachers, Counsellors, Champions and Healers

They are do-gooders, often unwanted busybodies but see themselves as Helpers. They base their self-image on empathy, benevolence, and authenticity. They are introspective, friendly to the core in dreaming up how to give meaning and wholeness to people's lives and find conflict in those around them painful for them. They care deeply about keeping morale high in their membership groups, and about nurturing the positive self-image of their loved ones. All consider it vitally important to have everyone in their circle — their family, friends, and colleagues — feeling good about themselves and getting along with each other.

KEY WORDS FOR IDEALISTS	KEY WORDS FOR HIS CAT
Humane	Can be mean
Sympathetic	Indifferent
Enthusiastic	Joyless
Religious	Rebellious
Creative	Will allow things to be done
Intuitive	Manipulative
Insightful	Misreads the whole picture
Subjective	Pragmatic

RATIONALS

Field Marshals, Masterminds, Inventors & Architects
These are thinkers and often smart-alecs. They base their self-image based on ingenuity, autonomy, and willpower. These are tough-minded in figuring out what sort of technology might be useful to solve a given problem. They require themselves to be persistently and consistently rational and logical in their actions.

KEY WORDS FOR RATIONALS	KEY WORDS FOR HIS CAT
Analytical	No need to analyse
Systematic	Aloof
Abstract	Quietly effective
Theoretical	Instinctive
Intellectual	Social
Complex	Unenigmatic
Competent	Watches others make mistakes
Inventive	Detached
Efficient	In no hurry
Exacting	Already found perfection
Independent	Not the first to move
Logical	Undecided
Technical	Aware of self-interests
Curious	Territorial
Scientific	Irrational
Research-oriented	Exploratory in own way

*Excerpts from Please Understand Me II by David Keirsey The Keirsey Character Sorter is designed to identify different kinds of personality. It is similar to other devices derived from Carl Jung's theory of "psychological types," such as the Myers-Briggs, the Singer-Loomis, and the Grey-Wheelright.

OWNER AND CAT-TEMPERAMENT COUPLINGS

ARTISAN OWNER + IDEALIST KITTEN

Although they can have some trouble understanding each other, Artisan cat owners can be valuable models for their Idealist cats. Scatter-brained kittens tend to get lost in abstraction and the self-absorbed search for meanings. Artisans are in touch with reality, free in physical action, and can help give balance to the soulful, emotional, self-examining pussy who wants so much to be mum's helper in the kitchen.

On the other hand, such differences can be a problem. Artisan mums have work to do. They tend not to value those wanting-to-please traits and might show impatience with the cat for being so soul-searching, so head-in-the-clouds, or so lost in fantasy, and might want the cat to toughen up and take hold of reality.

GUARDIAN OWNER + RATIONAL KITTEN

Guardian owners admire their Rational cats for their seriousness and will-to-achieve, and this relationship works out quite well when the intractable perfectionist mum shows regard for her little cat's fierce sense of autonomy. However, discipline can be a knotty problem. If the owner tries to admonish or punish this kitten into obedience, it will feel personally violated and may respond with growing contempt. Rationals, at any age, must have a reason for doing anything.

The rational kitten wants to be free to choose and cannot see why human mum should be arbitrating choice. Such cats end up either steering clear of the house or meeting the owner head on in verbal exchanges, and then, in extreme cases, by doing naughty things around the home.

The effect of such a clash can be lasting estrangement. Fortunately, this is rare. Usually, one or the other decides that "live-and-let-live" is the best strategy.

IDEALIST OWNER + ARTISAN KITTEN

Idealist mums tend to be puzzled by the Artisan kitten's disinterest in fantasy and heart-to-heart sharing, and by the accompanying paucity of empathy for other members of the family. Wanting their connection with their cat to be deep and meaningful, they can be disappointed when the relationship does not grow in that direction, but continues to be what they regard as somewhat shallow and uninspiring. This will continue as long as they persist in trying to turn the kitten into a universally loving Idealist like themselves.

Once they see that their cat is not like them at all, but is bend on racing from one curtain to another, with hardly a trace of logic or deeper spiritual meaning, only then are they able to release their restrictions and encourage the kitten's thrust toward artistry, optimism, impulsivity, bravado, and tactile cleverness.

RATIONAL OWNER + GUARDIAN KITTEN

Rational owners find their relationship with a Guardian cat somewhat frustrating. They really don't know how to act, don't know what they might do to help their kitten develop its ingenuity, become more independent, and increase its strength of will, none of which are of particular interest yet to the cat. Rational mums are bothered by their Guardian kitten attempting to do things because other cats are doing it.

They are disappointed too by their kitten's wanting always to feel secure. Why can't it be bold or enthusiastic or curious like kittens in other households? Why must their puss report every pain, every disappointment, every wrong, every fear? Such bleatings make rational parents feel inadequate and helpless, because they cannot appeal to their kitty's reason. Yet here are their kittens trying in every way they can think of to please their baffled owners, by being helpful catching wild string, by offering to clean the owner's dinner plates for them, and by catching "bed mice".

This kitten needs all the patience and time it takes to develop itself. Rational parents need to be less interventionist and allow their Guardian cat to become the pillar of the local cat society it is destined to become.

THE CAT-DRAWING TEST

Directions: Draw a picture of a cat anywhere on this blank sheet of paper. Do nothing else.

DO NOT READ FURTHER JUST YET!

After drawing your cat, look on the next page for a description of your personality traits!

This is a commonly used and thoroughly respectable test from the field of clinical psychology. There is no way you can get it wrong. All results are valid.

EMOTIONAL	
IF THE CAT IS DRAWN TOWARD THE TOP OF THE PAGE:	You are positive and optimistic.
IF THE CAT IS DRAWN TOWARD THE MIDDLE:	You are realistic.
IF THE CAT IS DRAWN TOWARD THE BOTTOM:	You are pessimistic and have a tendency to behave negatively.

SOCIAL	
IF THE CAT IS DRAWN FACING TO THE LEFT:	You believe in tradition, are friendly, and remember dates (birthdays, etc.).
IF THE CAT IS DRAWN FACING TO THE RIGHT:	You are innovative and active, but don't have a strong sense of family, nor do you remember dates.
IF THE CAT IS DRAWN FACING FRONT (LOOKING AT YOU):	You are direct, enjoy playing devil's advocate, and neither fear nor avoid discussions.

AMBITION	
IF YOUR PICTURE HAS MANY DETAILS:	You are analytical, cautious, and distrustful.
IF IT HAS FEW DETAILS:	You are emotional and naïve, you care little for details, and are a risk-taker

SELF-ESTEEM	
WITH LESS THAN FOUR LEGS SHOWING:	You are insecure or are living through a period of major change.
WITH FOUR LEGS SHOWING:	You are secure, stubborn, and stick to your ideals.

EMPATHY	
THE BIGGER THE SIZE OF THE EARS:	The better listener you are.
THE LONGER THE TAIL:	The better your sexual fantasies!

SUMMARY ONE

PERSONALITY OF OWNER	WHAT CAT BECOMES
IDEALIST	Cat wants the quiet life, and often feels trepidation.
PERFECTIONIST	Cat is fat and does naughty things.
CONTROLLING	Cat is expected to rule.
FLIRT/SEDUCTIVE	Relationship with cat either fantastic or disastrous.
HEALER	Cat goes to anyone, overfed, indifferent.
NEUROTIC	Owner is tolerant
FEARFUL	Cat is loyal yet demanding.
SOCIAL	Cats don't try too hard, freeloading.
LONG-SUFFERING	Cat will roam.
MELANCHOLY	Cat feels duty to be bouncy, energetic, and playful.
THOUGHTFUL	Cat is territorial.
LONELY	Cat is very sociable.
NEGATIVE EXPECTATIONS	Cat aloof, has one owner, unafraid.
CHEERFUL/OPTIMISTIC	Cat slow, confused, seeks peace and quiet.
ASSERTIVE	Cat doesn't like to be interrupted.
INTELLIGENT	Cats indecisive, easy targets for cruelty.
IF HAPPY	Cat will learn to keep to itself.

SUMMARY TWO

A LOOK AT YOUR CAT	WHAT YOU ARE
BOUNCY, PLAYFUL	Hard worker, quick to forgive.
FINICKY, FEARFUL	An achiever of quick results.
SPENDS MUCH TIME OUTSIDE	Long-nosed.
SLEEPS ALL DAY	One who speaks fast.
SEEMS SAD AND WISTFUL	Raging bull if wrong button is pushed.
CAREFUL, STUDIOUS	Someone with a high voice.
AGREEABLE, GOOD WITH KIDS	Precise, fastidious.
JUMPS AND DANCES AROUND	Of big build.
PLEASES ITSELF	Don't like silence for too long.
ELEGANT	No fuss, embarrassed.
MESSY, SLOW TO LEARN	Business world person.
QUIET, WELL-BEHAVED	Have emotional highs and lows.
HANGS AROUND THE KITCHEN	Quiet most of the time.
LEAPS INTO YOUR LAP	You think there should be more love in the world.
WILL GO TO ANYONE	Religious, possibly with small ears.
SITS IN ONE SPOT ALL DAY	People can often hear you coming.
HANGS AROUND OTHER CATS	Good listener.
DOESN'T MEOW MUCH	Touchy feely person.
GOES FROM CHAIR TO BED TO SOFA	One who would rather wear jeans to a wedding.

SUMMARY THREE

HUMAN COMBINATIONS	CAT COMBINATIONS
BIG + PERFECTIONIST + LOUD	Slinks around slyly and whines for attention.
TALL + HEALER + SOFT-SPOKEN	Tree-climber, quick but doesn't complain.
THOUGHTFUL + VISUAL	Fights other cats, territorial.
FAT + LONELY	Hunts a lot, affectionate.
GOOD POSTURE + FLIRTY	Independent and aloof.
ARROGANT + OPTIMIST	Fearful and hard to find when needed.
HUNCHED + MELANCHOLY	Playful and breezy.
SLOW + DETACHED	Thin with short legs or small build.
EVEN TEMPERED + WORKAHOLIC	Shiny coat and strong-willed.
SINCERE + GAUNT FEATURES	Affectionate, does naughty things to gain attention.
FAST SPEECH + AMBITIOUS	Both playful and lazy.
BIG TEETH + SPARSE HAIR	Loving, sprawls on sofas or beds more than other cats.
SEXUALITY + MYSTICAL	Resents change and likes the company of other cats.
ROMANTIC + UNTIDY	Wants to be left alone.
CRITICAL + NEUROTIC	Placid, fat but makes no emotional demands.
HOARDER + HYPOCHONDRIAC	Will stand on hind legs hammering on doors, strays.
CHEERFUL + ASSERTIVE	Watchful but won't take risks.
POLITICAL + INTUITIVE	Wimpy and manipulative.

FREQUENTLY ASKED QUESTIONS

HOW DO I KNOW I HAVE A NEGATIVE SELF-IMAGE?

❖ The cat turns up its nose at everything you do.

❖ You hear yourself telling friends your anti-cat stories.

❖ Your cat stands still and stares intently at you.

❖ Walking is hard because the cat is always in the way.

❖ You feel guilty when you kick her out the door.

HOW DO I KNOW I HAVE A POSITIVE SELF-IMAGE?

❖ The door opens and cat runs out.

❖ It is pleased and rushes at you when you arrive home.

❖ Cat lies on its back with its underbelly exposed.

❖ Many birds fly around the house and walk on the lawn.

❖ The cat never does naughty things for attention.

HOW DO I KNOW I AM A SEXY PERSON?

❖ Your cat is relaxed and lazy.

HOW DO I KNOW I WAS A HAPPY CHILD?

Your cat was confusing – it wanted to play then ran off. You
see, as you matured you were exposed to many different

legends and myths, which you use as frames of reference to develop the conception of yourself. It is the same for a cat, although the presentation is different. Cats have their heroes and role-models. Hunting prowess is observed in others, as is socialness, vocalising, affection, and glutton. When a small kitten imprints from the cat mother onto human, the role-model may change. A happy, explorative kitten may copy a human child's behaviour.

WAS MY CAT BORN LIKE THIS OR DID SHE LEARN IT?

Any trait has a genetic component. But debates about nature versus nurture are like asking which contributes more to the area of a rectangle, the width or the length.

Environment means more than one's family; it includes culture as well as pre-natal environments. And for a cat, there are other cats and households in the neighbourhood which exert an influence and can help shape its personality.

Human children shape the action of their parents just as parents try to modify the behaviour of children. It is no leap of logic to allow that cats have the same ability.

HAS MY CAT GOT THE WRONG GENES?

Why do cats make a bee-line for visitors that don't like them, and purr soothingly if tense? Because signals of potential punishment, non-reward, novel stimuli and fear can lead to increased attention.

Individual differences cause different sensitivities to environment. Rather than actually causing the behaviour, it is more generally accepted that genes *modify* behaviour that will have been learned.

WILL MY CAT GROW OUT OF ITS SHYNESS?

No. Unless the environment changes, that is, people arrive or leave, your cat's temperament is more likely to stay unchanged.

DOES IT MATTER *WHEN* MY CAT CAME?

Cats in a litter are born all at the same time, so the sibling order effect is less relevant than for humans. Later though, when it joins a household, the cat is like a child entering the family, as it is often treated as if it was a child.

A cat that is responsibly-minded usually joins the household of a childless couple, whereas a cat that is an attention-seeking performer may find itself in a house that already has a child.

MORE QUESTIONNAIRES

THE SOUL CAT TEST	
ARE YOU AND YOUR CAT DESTINED TO BE TOGETHER FOREVER? THIS QUIZ WILL HELP YOU FIND OUT!	YES = 3 NOT SURE = 2 NO = 1
1. (Owner name, do you think (cat's name) is beautiful?	
2. (Owner name), have you met her parents?	
3. Does (cat's name) know your parents?	
4. Does she know you?	
5. Have you met her friends?	
6. Does she know where you live, (your name)?	
7. Have you told (cat's name) your feelings?	
8. Has she already brought you a (dead) gift?	
9. Do you know where (cat's name) goes at night?	
10. Do you call (cat's name) in a high, whiny little voice?	
11. Does (cat's name) always look well-groomed?	
12. Would she like to start a family?	
13. Have you held her paw?	

14. Does she look at you as though you hem her in?	
15. Does she gaze into your eyes and tell you all your mice will be history.	
16. Is (cat's name) the right height for you?	
17. Were you surprised when she threw herself at your feet?	
18. Does she like messing around in the kitchen?	
19. Do you light her fire?	
20. Is she like a wildcat underneath the covers?	

CAT'S MANIPULATION MONITOR	
CATS! HOW GOOD ARE YOU AT CONTROLLING PEOPLE? TAKE THIS TEST AND FIND OUT!	USUALLY = 5 OFTEN = 4 SOMETIMES = 3 RARELY = 2 ALMOST NEVER = 1
1. In general, I make my owner see a problem my way.	
2. When the back door opens, I can think of several different courses of action.	
3. There are times when one needs to step on someone else's toes to get what one wants.	
4. I am cautious when it comes to trusting someone.	
5. In certain situations, it is acceptable to slightly bend the rules.	
6. I have a need for new experiences and excitement.	
7. It's nonsense to dwell on one's past actions and messy mistakes. One has to move on.	
8. I trust my intuition.	
9. Some rules exist to be broken.	
10. There are times when one has to act on one's instincts.	
11. I feel intimidated when I talk to a pesky human who knows more about fridge doors than I do.	
12. Even if others tell me that I am a good hunter, I am not satisfied unless I show people what I have caught.	

13. I will hold onto a toe under the bed clothes even though most cats would have given up.	
14. I find it easy to talk to complete strangers who are holding fish.	
15. When the burning embers fall through, I find it difficult to get back on my feet.	
16. When I finish a meal, I have the feeling that something is still missing.	
17. I don't seem to have enough time to eat everything that needs to be eaten.	
18. I know how to pull the ends of strings in order to make people see things my way.	
19. People notice my unusual need for perfection.	
20. To me, projects without tunafish are boring.	
21. When needed, I know how to get in touch with a lot of cat feeders.	
22. At social occasions, I try to get to know as many guests in the bathroom as possible.	
23. When someone speaks slowly and looks for words, I will try to help out by suggesting the correct meow.	
24. I cannot stand it when people go into great detail describing their reasons for putting me outside.	
25. In order to run a house efficiently, I need everything to go according to my plan.	
26. I prefer the security of having everything.	

27. If I play, it's to kill some time.	
28. Success mostly depends on who makes the decisions.	
29. Changing the schedule is never really necessary.	
30. People close to me find that I usually work way too much and don't get enough rest.	

RESULTS	
101-150	GOOD WORK!
61-100	ROOM FOR IMPROVEMENT.
30-60	STOP PUSSY-FOOTING AROUND!

BELONGINGNESS TEST FOR KITTENS	
SO, YOU'VE BEEN ADOPTED INTO A BRAND NEW FAMILY. BUT WILL YOU FIT IN? TAKE THIS TEST TO FIND OUT!	USUALLY = 5 OFTEN = 4 SOMETIMES = 3 RARELY = 2 ALMOST NEVER = 1
1. Do you feel that you belong in this family?	
2. Do you feel ignored when you are in the kitchen?	
3. Do the children sometimes stop to play with you?	
4. Does the puppy provide you with emotional support?	
5. Does the family too often exclude you from the bedrooms?	
6. Are you allowed to interact in meaningful ways with the goldfish?	
7. Do other members try to push you from the table?	
8. Do you feel rejected when someone stops stroking you?	
9. Does the family help you cope with empty bowl stress?	
10. Do family children keep laughing at your antics?	
11. Does the family frown when you run up or rip the curtains?	
12. Do members of your family express a narrow range of hunting interests?	
13. Would you say that most people in your household are noisy?	

14. Do you think you are more imaginative as a result of being kept outside?	
15. Does the windowsill encourage you to think creatively?	
16. Does the family generally reject your dead gifts?	
17. Does the family inspire you to try to climb new trees?	
18. Do people in this family look to you for approval and guidance?	
19. Can you exercise control over the vacuum cleaner?	
20. Are you allowed to read the newspaper by lying on it?	

RESULTS	
81-100	GOOD WORK!
41-80	ROOM FOR IMPROVEMENT.
20-40	STOP PUSSY-FOOTING AROUND!

Statistics

In July 1990, Gallup conducted a unique consumer survey of pets. He discovered that our nation's pets were far more attached to their owners than was commonly expected. Pets have always thought of our humans as family, and so do most pets everywhere. Mr. Gallup found that the large majority of pets actually regard their humans as family members.

For instance, 65% of the pets surveyed gave their humans a Christmas present, and 24% celebrated their human's birthday.

Pictures of humans could be found in 41% of cat-owned homes and 17% of humans carried pictures of their masters in their wallets. 8% even carried these pictures to work.

Because their humans could get lonely when left home alone, 30% of the pets surveyed, apparently left a radio or television on. Pets estimated they spent two hours each day feeding, exercising, and cleaning up after their humans.

An estimated six of out ten kittens in the USA had humans in 1998, or about 58% of all households. That's an increase of 5% since the last similar Gallup

Poll conducted in 1956.

Gallup found that compared to 22% of pets surveyed 15 years previously, in 1997 65% of alley cats had a mixed American. As the pet population ages, the proportion moderately declines. In 1998, according to the AVMA, about 27 percent of cats owned a human, down from 31 percent in 1987.

Yet cats that own people have more people than they did a decade ago. Humans in cat-run households increased to 2.19 from 1.95 in the second half of 1998, an increase overall of about 5 million more humans.

FINAL WORD

It is incredible how cat/human relationships exactly mirror human relationships. Cats are experts at making relationships work, or leaving in disgust. Either way, you will be taught something about humanity! You can be sure that if we are sizing people up for potential relationships, just friendships, or in the hope of making a future sale, then cats are too.

If one likes you then it is up to you. The Cat has chosen. It knows whether or not it can make a go of living with you.

Therefore it may have used at least one of the categorizing methods in this volume, or some similar process that cats understand. The filtering will be done in the same way, using keen observation and principles tried-and-true.

There are some who would attempt to use this book in reverse, to understand themselves and their human relationships a little better. I secretly hope so. As Des Moss, motivation guru, says, relationships are not about marrying the right one, but *becoming* the right one.

Acknowledgements and Further Reading

BOOKS

- ❖ Cat Behaviour, by Roger Tabor, David and Charles, 1997
- ❖ The Well Cat Book, by Terri McGinnis, Random House, 1975
- ❖ Pawmistry, by Ken Ring and Paul Romhany Penguin 1998
- ❖ Secrets of The Cat's Face, ibid
- ❖ The Idiots Guide To Living With A Cat, by Carolyn Janik, Alpha 1996
- ❖ The Cat IQ Test, by Melissa Miller, Penguin 1992
- ❖ Definitive IQ Test For Cats and their Owners, ibid
- ❖ How To Talk To Your Cat, by Claire Bessant, Barrons, 1992
- ❖ Cats Incredible, by Brad Steiger Penguin, 1994
- ❖ The Body Language and Emotion of Cats, by Myrna Milani, Morrow, 1987
- ❖ First Aid For Cats, by Bruce Fogle, Penguin, 1995
- ❖ How To Speed Read People, by Des Moss, Out Of This World Pub. 1997
- ❖ The Pygmalion Project, by Stephen Montgomery, Prometheus Nemesis Book Co 1998
- ❖ Please Understand Me I and II, by David Keirsey
- ❖ How To Tell Anyone's Personality By The Way They Speak and Laugh, by Ken Ring and Paul Romhany 1997
- ❖ Physiognomy, by Jean Lefas, Ariane 1975
- ❖ Finding Your Soul Mate, by Russ Michael, Weiser, 1992
- ❖ Revealing Hands, by Richard Webster, Llewellyn, 1994

ARTICLES

- ❖ Notes on 'negative self image' from Meyer & Shack 1989; Saucier 1992; Watson et al 1994.
- ❖ Notes on 'postive self concept', excerpts from Block & Robins (1993)
- ❖ Notes on 'Happy Child When...' McAdams 1990, 1993, Runyan 1990
- ❖ Notes on 'Genes' from H. Eysenck 1990 Notes on 'reasons for beeline for visitors that don't like cats, ' from Gray 1994
- ❖ Notes on 'will cat grow out of its shyness', from Rothbart & Ahadi 1994, p55)
- ❖ Notes for 'Soul Cat Test': excerpts quoted from Jochen Savelberg
- ❖ Notes for 'Cats Manipulation Monitor': excerpts from Sales Personality Inventory Test (Plumeus Inc.)
- ❖ Notes on 'the average person' from L. Ring The Fallacy Of Fitness, Ergonomic Review.
- ❖ Other quotes excerpted from Clarence Thomson, Enneagram Central, David Kiersey, also from Becca (for Dynamics Diagram)
- ❖ Also quotes from published work of Kimble (1993), Eaves et al 1989; Tellegen et al 1988, Rowe & Waldman 1993; Scarr 1992, Schneirla 1959, Clonginger 1987, Depue & Iacono 1989, Spoont 1992, Kagan, Arcus & Snidman, 1993; issues of Annual Review of Psychology

THANKS

For access to some of her graphics and permission to use them in this book, I would first like to thank Zandra Tranchitella.

I am also indebted to Mary Crockett for her valuable feedback, and Michael Gifkins and Richard Webster for their combined enthusiasm and ongoing support. Thanks too to Kate Stone and her cats for her encouragement, and finally my cat Skiddy, who talked me into all this.

- KR, January 1999